AF575229

Design Annual 2002

My work is about images, not about technique. In the first place that's simply my character. But it's also a way of making up for my lack of training. I never finished high school or the art academy, so I could never beat my competitors at technique. And if you can't be better, you have to be different, even outrageous. If everybody is doing pantomime, I do pantomime with song!

Bei meiner Arbeit geht es um Bilder, nicht um Technik. Erstens entspricht das meiner Natur, und zweitens kompensiere ich damit den Mangel an Ausbildung. Ich habe keinen höheren Schulabschluss und wurde aus der Kunstakademie geworfen, deshalb konnte ich die Konkurrenz nie mit technischen Mitteln schlagen. Wenn man nicht besser als andere sein kann, muss man anders sein, notfalls auch schamlos. Wenn jeder Pantomime macht – stumm, wie es sich gehört –, mache ich Pantomime mit Gesang!

Mon travail se concentre sur les images et non pas sur la technique. S'il en est ainsi, c'est en raison de mon tempérament. Mais c'est aussi une façon de compenser mon manque de savoir-faire. Au lycée comme à l'Ecole des beaux-arts, je me suis arrêté en cours de route et, au plan technique, je n'ai jamais pu surpasser mes rivaux. Et si l'on n'est pas à même de faire mieux, autant faire quelque chose de différent, voire d'outrageant… Si tout le monde fait du pantomime, et bien moi, je fais du pantomime en chantant! Anthon Beeke

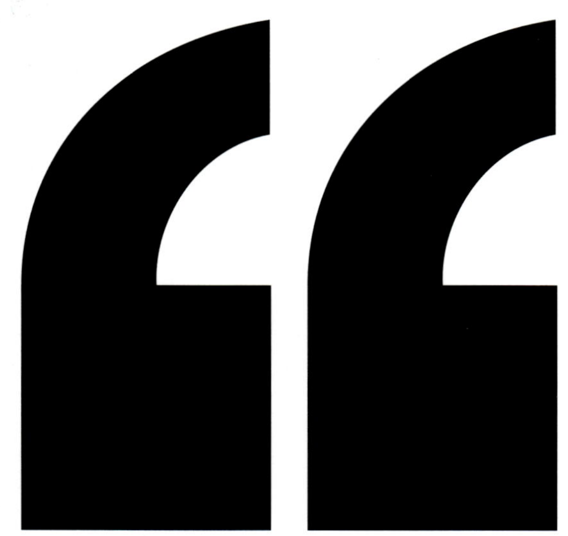

I always think of Alan Fletcher at Pentagram…sitting at a table by himself with a bottle of wine, sketching a squashed Coke can pinned to a board behind him—playing. It feels to me like the playfulness of design has been taken over by the business side, and that there are more and more commercial restraints.

Ich sehe noch immer Alan Fletcher vor mir,...er sitzt allein am Tisch, vor sich eine Flasche Wein, und zeichnet eine zerdrückte Cola-Dose, die hinter ihm an der Wand befestigt ist – er spielt. Ich habe das Gefühl, dass die wirtschaftlichen Aspekte das Spielerische am Design ausgemerzt haben, dass es immer mehr ökonomisch bedingte Einschränkungen gibt.

Je revois toujours cette image d'Alan Fletcher chez Pentagram, assis seul à une table, une bouteille de vin posée devant lui. Il est en train d'esquisser une boîte de Coca écrasée dont l'original est fixé au mur, dans son dos – il s'amuse, tout simplement. Il me semble que les considérations d'ordre économique l'ont emporté sur l'aspect ludique du design. Il est difficile de faire fi des contraintes financières toujours plus pesantes. Vince Frost

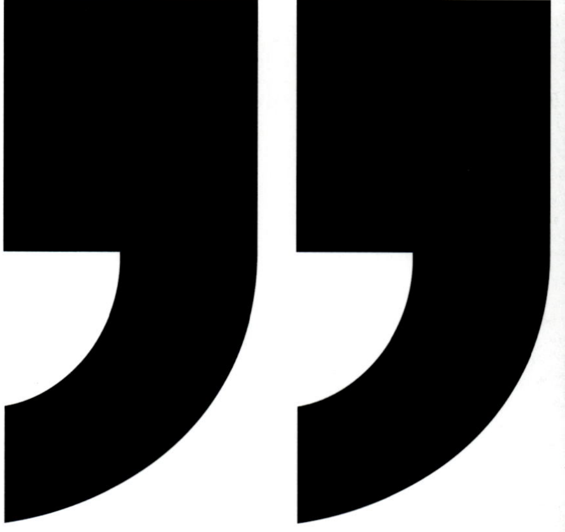

(this spread) Design Firm **Pentagram Design** Art Director **Michael Gericke** Designers **Michael Gericke** and **Su Matthews** Client **Loews Cineplex**

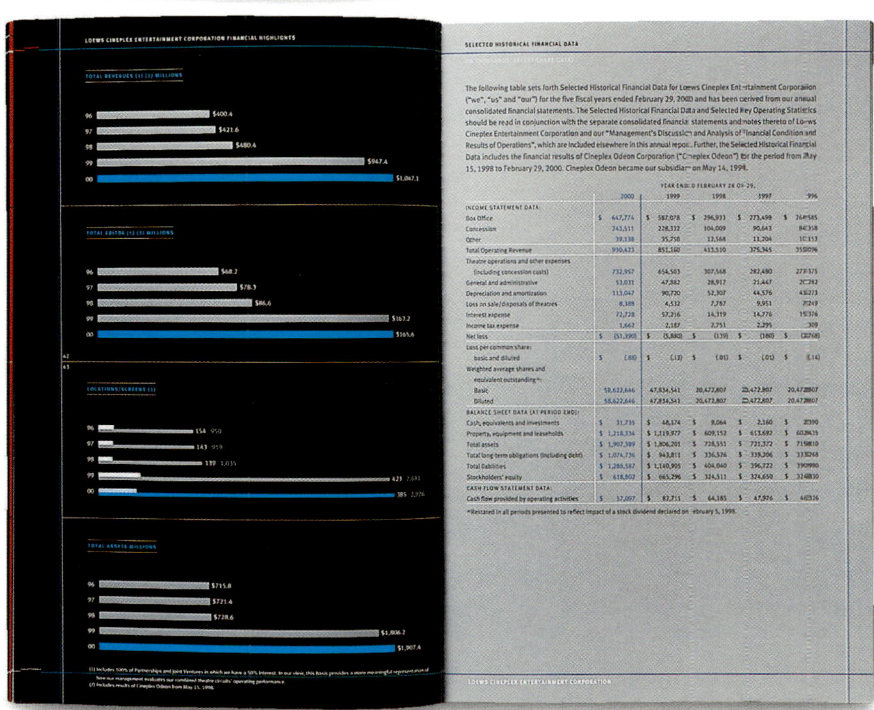

SELECTED HISTORICAL FINANCIAL DATA

The following table sets forth Selected Historical Financial Data for Loews Cineplex Entertainment Corporation ("we", "us" and "our") for the five fiscal years ended February 29, 2000 and has been derived from our annual consolidated financial statements. The Selected Historical Financial Data and Selected Key Operating Statistics should be read in conjunction with the separate consolidated financial statements and notes thereto of Loews Cineplex Entertainment Corporation and our "Management's Discussion and Analysis of Financial Condition and Results of Operations", which are included elsewhere in this annual report. Further, the Selected Historical Financial Data includes the financial results of Cineplex Odeon Corporation ("Cineplex Odeon") for the period from May 15, 1998 to February 29, 2000. Cineplex Odeon became our subsidiary on May 14, 1998.

	YEAR ENDED FEBRUARY 28 OR 29,				
	2000	1999	1998	1997	1996
INCOME STATEMENT DATA:					
Box Office	$ 647,774	$ 587,078	$ 296,933	$ 273,498	$ 264,585
Concession	243,511	228,332	104,009	90,643	84,358
Other	39,138	35,750	12,568	11,204	10,153
Total Operating Revenue	930,423	851,160	413,510	375,345	359,096
Theatre operations and other expenses (including concession costs)	732,957	654,503	307,568	282,480	277,375
General and administrative	53,031	47,882	28,917	21,447	20,282
Depreciation and amortization	113,047	90,720	52,307	44,576	41,273
Loss on sale/disposals of theatres	8,389	4,532	7,787	9,951	7,249
Interest expense	72,728	57,216	14,319	14,776	15,376
Income tax expense	1,662	2,187	2,751	2,295	309
Net loss	$ (51,390)	$ (5,880)	$ (139)	$ (180)	$ (2,768)
Loss per common share: basic and diluted	$ (.88)	$ (.12)	$ (.01)	$ (.01)	$ (.14)
Weighted average shares and equivalent outstanding*:					
Basic	58,622,646	47,834,541	20,472,807	20,472,807	20,472,807
Diluted	58,622,646	47,834,541	20,472,807	20,472,807	20,472,807
BALANCE SHEET DATA (AT PERIOD END):					
Cash, equivalents and investments	$ 31,735	$ 48,174	$ 9,064	$ 2,160	$ 2,390
Property, equipment and leaseholds	$ 1,218,334	$ 1,119,977	$ 609,152	$ 613,692	$ 602,435
Total assets	$ 1,907,389	$ 1,806,201	$ 728,551	$ 721,372	$ 715,810
Total long-term obligations (including debt)	$ 1,074,736	$ 943,811	$ 336,576	$ 339,206	$ 333,268
Total liabilities	$ 1,288,587	$ 1,140,905	$ 404,040	$ 396,722	$ 390,980
Stockholders' equity	$ 618,802	$ 665,296	$ 324,511	$ 324,650	$ 324,830
CASH FLOW STATEMENT DATA:					
Cash flow provided by operating activities	$ 57,097	$ 82,711	$ 64,185	$ 47,976	$ 40,326

*Restated in all periods presented to reflect impact of a stock dividend declared on February 5, 1998.

LOEWS CINEPLEX ENTERTAINMENT CORPORATION

Design Firm **Weymouth Design** Art Director **Bob Kellerman** Designer **Kerry LaCoste** Photographer **Mike Weymouth** Illustrator **Leslie Bistrowitz** Copywriters **Susan Klein, Courier Corporation** and **Weymouth Design** Client **Courier Corporation**

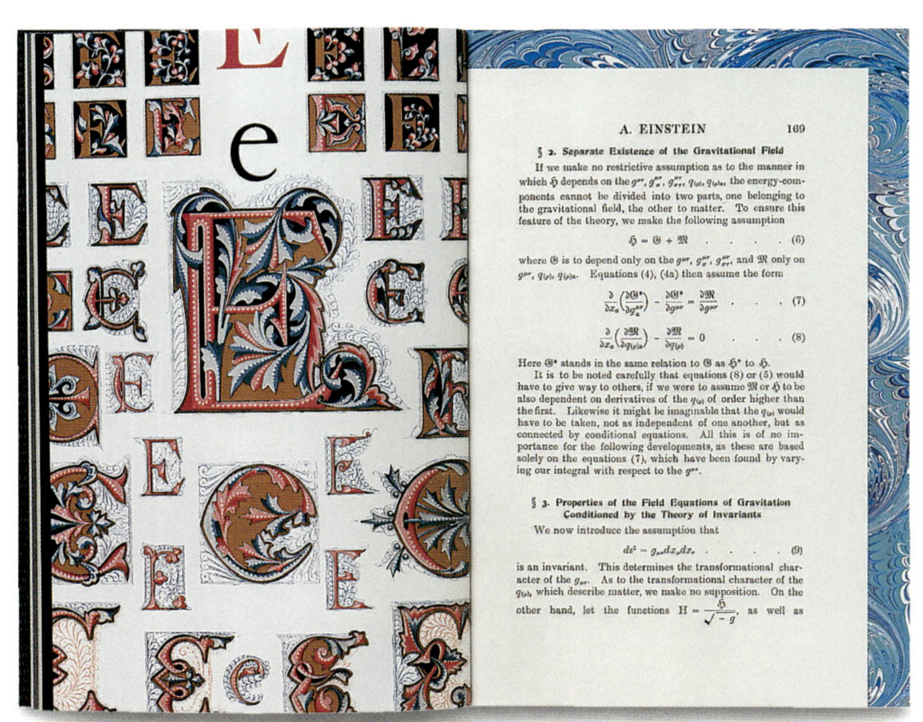

A. EINSTEIN 169

§ 2. Separate Existence of the Gravitational Field

If we make no restrictive assumption as to the manner in which $\mathfrak{H}$ depends on the $g^{\mu\nu}$, $g^{\mu\nu}_{\sigma}$, $g^{\mu\nu}_{\sigma\tau}$, $q_{(\rho)}$, $q_{(\rho)\alpha}$, the energy-components cannot be divided into two parts, one belonging to the gravitational field, the other to matter. To ensure this feature of the theory, we make the following assumption

$$\mathfrak{H} = \mathfrak{G} + \mathfrak{M} \quad . \quad . \quad . \quad . \quad (6)$$

where $\mathfrak{G}$ is to depend only on the $g^{\mu\nu}$, $g^{\mu\nu}_{\sigma}$, $g^{\mu\nu}_{\sigma\tau}$, and $\mathfrak{M}$ only on $g^{\mu\nu}$, $q_{(\rho)}$, $q_{(\rho)\alpha}$. Equations (4), (4a) then assume the form

$$\frac{\partial}{\partial x_\alpha}\left(\frac{\partial \mathfrak{G}^*}{\partial g^{\mu\nu}_\alpha}\right) - \frac{\partial \mathfrak{G}^*}{\partial g^{\mu\nu}} = \frac{\partial \mathfrak{M}}{\partial g^{\mu\nu}} \quad . \quad . \quad . \quad (7)$$

$$\frac{\partial}{\partial x_\alpha}\left(\frac{\partial \mathfrak{M}}{\partial q_{(\rho)\alpha}}\right) - \frac{\partial \mathfrak{M}}{\partial q_{(\rho)}} = 0 \quad . \quad . \quad . \quad (8)$$

Here $\mathfrak{G}^*$ stands in the same relation to $\mathfrak{G}$ as $\mathfrak{H}^*$ to $\mathfrak{H}$.

It is to be noted carefully that equations (8) or (5) would have to give way to others, if we were to assume $\mathfrak{M}$ or $\mathfrak{H}$ to be also dependent on derivatives of the $q_{(\rho)}$ of order higher than the first. Likewise it might be imaginable that the $q_{(\rho)}$ would have to be taken, not as independent of one another, but as connected by conditional equations. All this is of no importance for the following developments, as these are based solely on the equations (7), which have been found by varying our integral with respect to the $g^{\mu\nu}$.

§ 3. Properties of the Field Equations of Gravitation Conditioned by the Theory of Invariants

We now introduce the assumption that

$$ds^2 = g_{\mu\nu}dx_\mu dx_\nu \quad . \quad . \quad . \quad . \quad (9)$$

is an invariant. This determines the transformational character of the $g_{\mu\nu}$. As to the transformational character of the $q_{(\rho)}$, which describe matter, we make no supposition. On the other hand, let the functions $H = \frac{\mathfrak{H}}{\sqrt{-g}}$, as well as

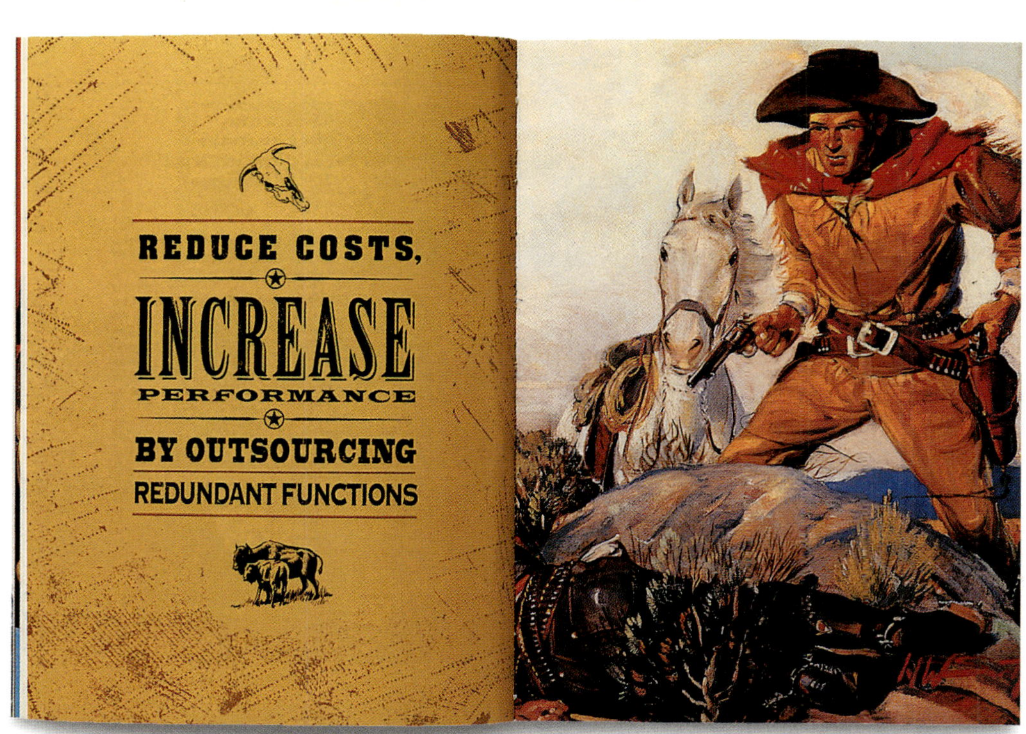

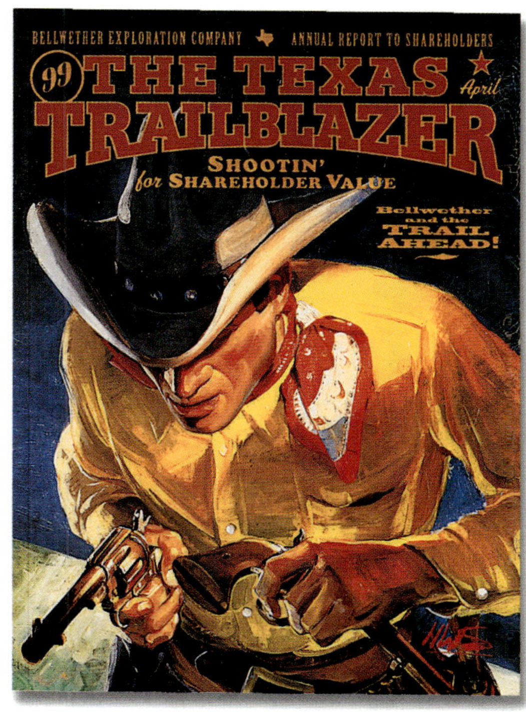

Consolidated Balance Sheets

ASSETS (Amounts in thousands)	December 31, 1999	December 31, 1998
CURRENT ASSETS:		
Cash and cash equivalents	$ 6,101	$ 10
Accounts receivable and accrued revenues	14,354	15,602
Accounts receivable – related parties	-	853
Prepaid expenses	1,562	1,719
Total current assets	22,017	18,184
PROPERTY, PLANT AND EQUIPMENT, AT COST:		
Oil and gas properties (full cost):		
United States – Unproved properties of $16,325 and $8,754 excluded from amortization as of December 31, 1999 and 1998 respectively	344,778	289,040
Latin America – Unproved properties of $404 and $191 excluded from amortization as of December 31, 1999 and 1998, respectively	1,246	191
Gas plant facilities	17,775	17,406
	363,799	306,637
Less accumulated depreciation, depletion and amortization	(227,226)	(198,421)
	136,573	108,216
INVESTMENT IN OUTSIDE COMPANIES	4,554	-
DEFERRED INCOME TAXES	2,739	-
OTHER ASSETS	5,878	4,796
	$ 171,761	$ 131,196
CURRENT LIABILITIES:		
Accounts payable and accrued liabilities	$ 18,247	$ 11,982
Accounts payable – related parties	-	125
Total current liabilities	18,247	12,107
LONG TERM DEBT	130,000	104,400
OTHER LIABILITIES	200	200
STOCKHOLDERS' EQUITY:		
Preferred stock, $0.01 par value, 1,000,000 shares authorized, none issued or outstanding	-	-
Common stock, $0.01 par value, 30,000,000 shares authorized 14,168,791 and 14,164,791 shares issued at December 31, 1999, and 1998, respectively	142	142
Additional paid in capital	80,455	80,442
Retained earnings (deficit)	(55,378)	(64,191)
Treasury stock, at cost, 311,000 and 310,800 shares at December 31, 1999 and 1998, respectively	(1,905)	(1,904)
Total stockholders' equity	23,314	14,489
	$ 171,761	$ 131,196

See Notes to Consolidated Financial Statements

Statements of Operations

(Amounts in thousands, except per share data)	Year Ended December 31, 1999	Year Ended December 31, 1998	Six Month Transition Period Ended December 31, 1997	Fiscal Year Ended June 30, 1997
REVENUES:				
Gas revenues	$41,380	$ 46,461	$26,755	$24,202
Oil revenues	26,568	26,756	17,408	14,865
Gas plant revenues, net	1,464	1,203	804	3,330
Interest and other income	1,335	1,347	609	363
	70,747	75,767	45,576	42,760
COSTS AND EXPENSES:				
Production expenses	21,532	25,381	13,836	11,437
General and administrative expenses	7,848	8,459	3,748	4,042
Depreciation, depletion and Amortization	23,863	39,688	16,352	15,574
Impairment expense	–	73,899	-	-
Interest expense	11,845	11,660	5,978	4,477
	65,088	159,087	39,914	35,530
Income (loss) before income tax (benefit)	5,659	(83,320)	5,662	7,230
Provision for income tax (benefit)	(3,154)	(6,069)	2,114	2,585
Net income (loss)	$ 8,813	$ (77,251)	$ 3,548	$ 4,645
Net income(loss) per share	$ .64	$ (5.50)	$ .26	$ 0.46
Net income(loss) per share – diluted	$ .63	$ (5.50)	$ .25	$ 0.45
Weighted average common shares outstanding	13,854	14,039	13,876	10,201
Weighted average common shares outstanding – diluted	13,896	14,039	14,446	10,261

See Notes to Consolidated Financial Statements

Design Firm **Squires & Company** Creative Director and Designer **Brandon Murphy** Illustrators **Mark Zingarecci** and **Tom Lea** Copywriter **Bill Baldwin** Client **Bellwether Exploration Company**

Design Firm **Turner & Associates** Creative Director **Steve Turner** Designer **Laurie Garrigan** Client **Yahoo!**

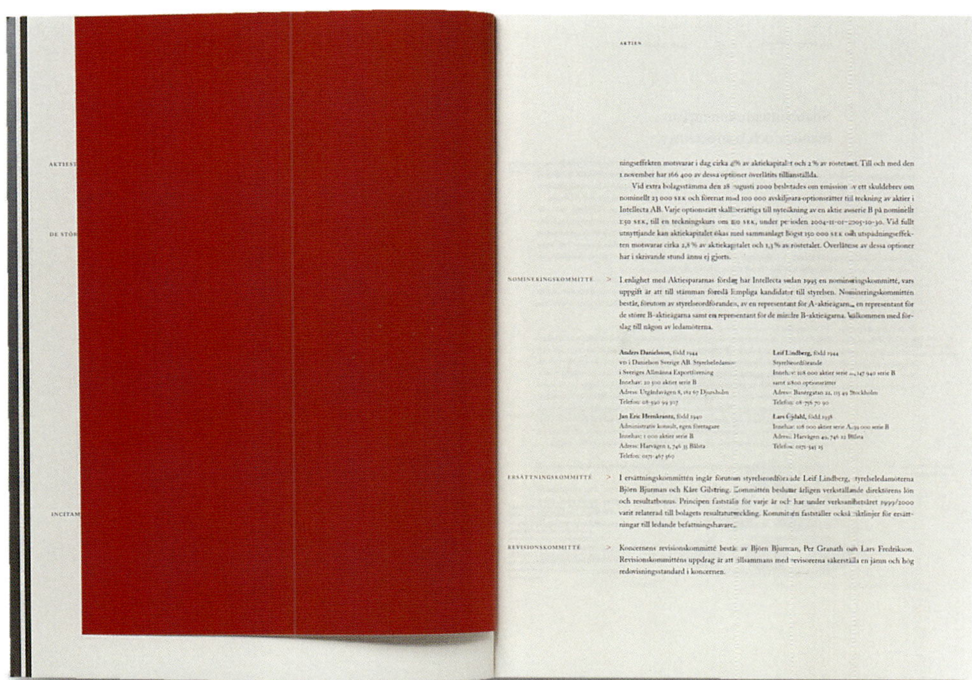

AKTIEN

AKTIESTRUKTUR

AKTIESLAG	ANTAL AKTIER	ANTAL RÖSTER	ANDEL AV KAPITAL, %	ANDEL AV RÖSTER, %
serie A*, 10 röster	432 000	4 320 000	10,3	53,5
serie B, 1 röst	3 756 269	3 756 269	89,7	46,5
Summa	4 188 269	8 076 269	100,0	100,0

** Hembudsskyldighet följer för A-aktien*

DE STÖRSTA ÄGARNA

AKTIER ENLIGT VPC 2000-10-31	INNEHAV A-AKTIER	INNEHAV B-AKTIER	PROCENT AV KAPITAL	PROCENT AV RÖSTER
Richard Ohlson *(privat och via bolag)*		321 000	7,7	4,0
Lars Peder Hedberg *(via bolag)*		263 500	6,3	3,3
Leif Lindberg	108 000	147 940	6,1	15,2
Lars Fredrikson	108 000	123 260	5,5	14,9
Eskil Johannesson		225 300	5,3	2,8
Lars Öjdahl	108 000	39 000	3,5	13,9
Hans Liljeberg	108 000	12 460	2,9	13,5
Olle Lindberg		119 090	2,9	1,5
Lars Lindberg		107 600	2,6	1,3
Banco Småbolagsfond		106 800	2,6	1,3
LF Wasa Småbolagsfonden		56 000	1,3	0,7
Annika Johannesson		50 000	1,2	0,6
David Fredriksson		44 440	1,1	0,5
Yngve Sundin		40 525	1,0	0,5
Kristofer Fredriksson		38 436	0,9	0,5
Eva Anell		34 600	0,8	0,4
Peter Stigwan		31 200	0,8	0,4
Bengt Jutendahl		30 400	0,7	0,4
Bo Larsson		29 600	0,7	0,4
Övriga		1 935 118	46,1	23,9
Totalt	432 000	3 756 269	100,0	100,0

INCITAMENTSPROGRAM

Som ett led i Intellectas incitamentsprogram för anställda i bolaget och dotterbolag har bolaget utgett två skuldebrev med avskiljbara optionsrätter till teckning av aktier i Intellecta.

Vid extra bolagsstämma den 15 oktober 1998 beslutades om emission av ett skuldebrev om nominellt 10 000 SEK och förenat med 176 000 *(justerat efter split 4:1)* avskiljbara optionsrätter till teckning av aktier i Intellecta AB. Varje optionsrätt skall berättiga till nyteckning av en aktie av serie B på nominellt 1:50 SEK, till en teckningskurs om 62:15 SEK, under perioden 2002-11-01–2003-11-01. Vid fullt utnyttjande kan aktiekapitalet ökas med sammanlagt högst 264 000 SEK och utspäd-

Design Firm **Intellecta Corporate** Art Director and Designer **Anders Schmidt** Photographers **Sue Bennet** and **Bruno Ehrs** Client **Intellecta AB**

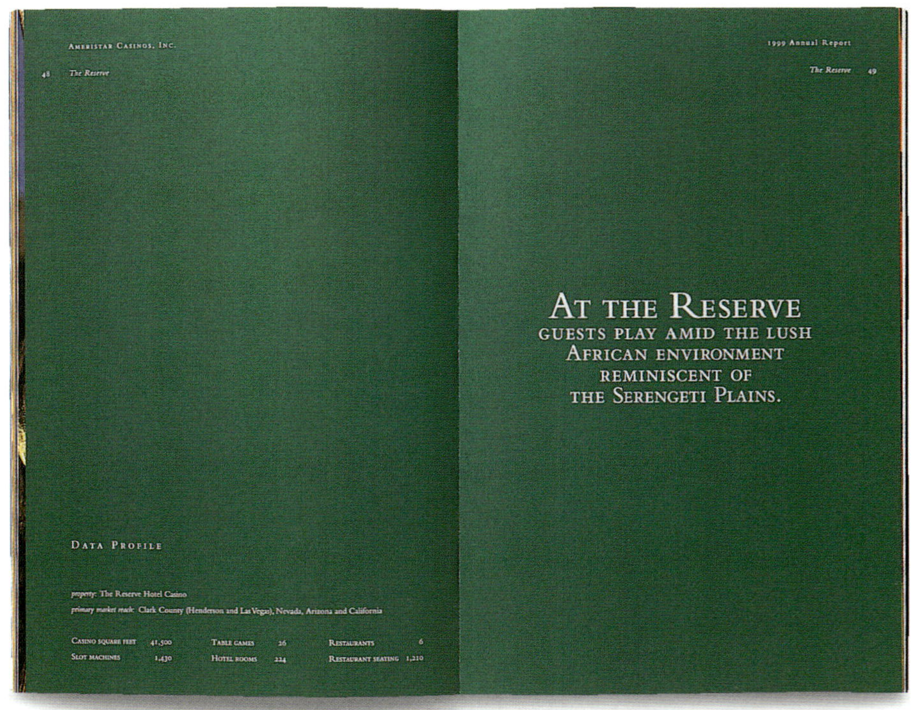

Design Firm **Oliver Kuhlmann** Creative and Art Director **Deanna Kuhlmann** Designer **Monica King** Photographer **Gregg Goldman** Copywriters **Penny Benda** and **Connie Wilson** Client **Ameristar Casinos**

Design Firm **Sibley Peteet Design** Art Directors and Designers **Rex Peteet** and **Carrie Eko** Illustrator **Peter Krämer** Copywriter **Doug Irving** Client **Tropical Sportswear International**

Design Firm **Weymouth Design** Art Director **Tom Laidlaw** Designer **Jonathan Grove** Photographers **Michael Weymouth** and **Brian Barnes** Client **Epix Medical**

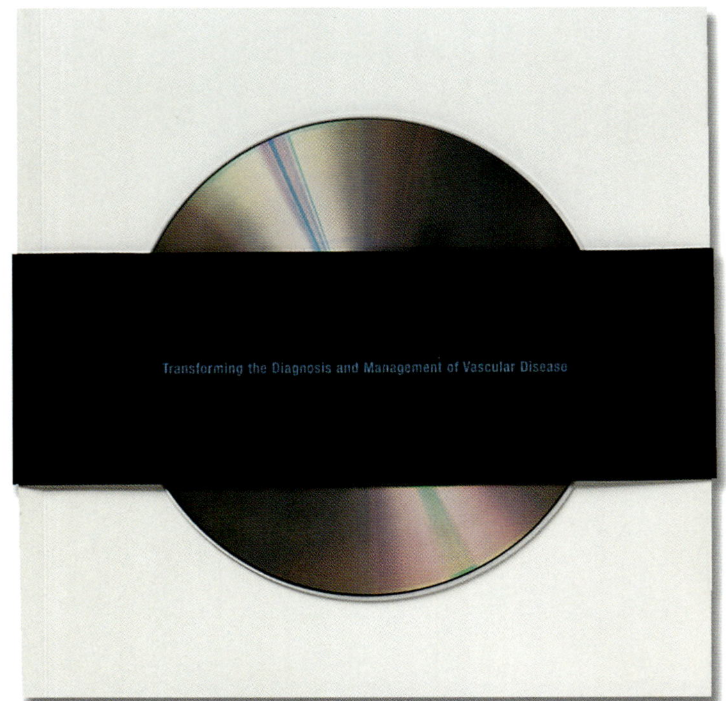

This patient's doctor has told her that she might have cardiovascular disease and will need to undergo an invasive, time-consuming and painful procedure called X-ray angiography to confirm her diagnosis. While X-ray angiograms are currently the standard in the field to definitively diagnose vascular disease, the process is associated with numerous clinical and technical drawbacks. We at EPIX believe that there's a better way to help this patient and the millions of people like her who have cardiovascular diseases.

The use of magnetic resonance imaging (MRI) would overcome many of the drawbacks associated with X-ray angiography and would provide physicians with what they have wanted for decades—to be able to apply MRI technology to vascular disease diagnosis and management. The Company's lead product in development, AngioMARK (MS-325), is emerging as an imaging agent that permits for the first time the practical application of MRI to vascular disease. By developing and commercializing AngioMARK for MRI, EPIX plans to transform the practice of vascular medicine.

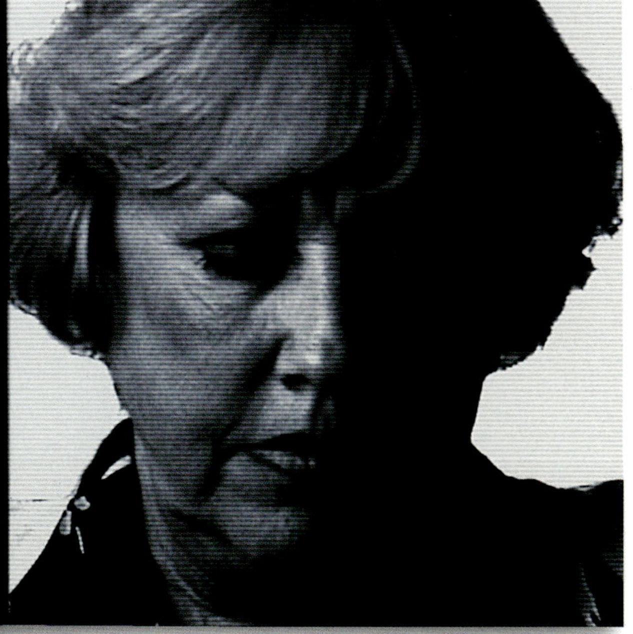

Design Firm **Turner & Associates** Creative Director **Steve Turner** Art Director **Phil Hamlett** Designer **Laura Milton** Photographer **Stephen Austin Welch** Copywriter **Jon Rant** Client **Macromedia, Inc.**

Design Firm **Taku Satoh Design Office Inc.** Art Director and Designer **Taku Satoh** Client **Japan Graphic Designers Association Inc.**

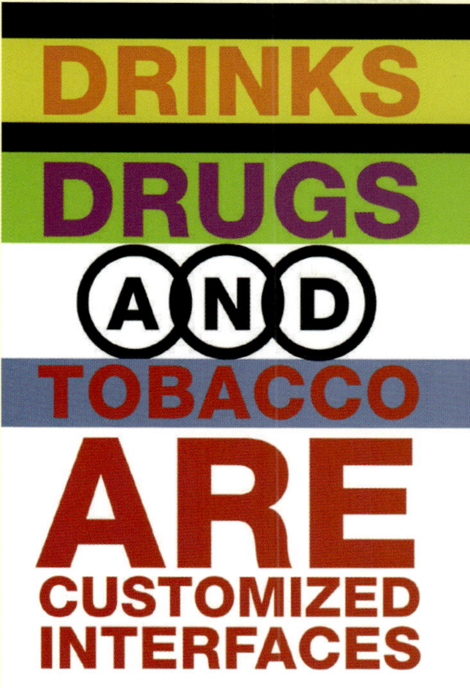

Design Firm **Mieke Gerritzen** Creative Director, Art Director and Designer **Mieke Gerritzen** Copywriters **Ted Byfield** and **Max Kisman**

JAPAN
2000
MARKETING
&
ADVERTISING
YEARBOOK

Design Firm **Montgomery & Pfeifer** Creative Directors **Dietmar Henneka** and **Liliane Lerch** Art Director **Urs Schwerzmann** Designers **Herbie Pfeifer** Copywriter **Martin Crellin** and **Dietmar Henneka** Client **DaimlerChrysler AG**

Design Firm **Taku Satoh Design Office Inc.** Art Director **Taku Satoh** Designer **Taku Satoh, Ichiji Ohishi, Shino Misawa** and **Takehiko Shimamura** Client **Tokyo Art Directors Club**

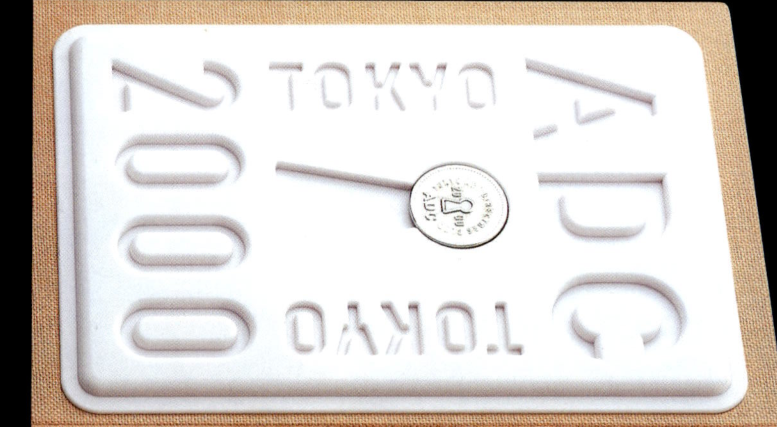

The first to settle here were not alone for long.

The middle Rio Grande Valley has embraced the native and newcomer alike.

Settlers trickled in from the East,

bearing bricks, clapboards and peaked roofs

to take root amongst the native rounded corners

and shaded *portales*.

Highrise now overlooks *hacienda*,

and asphalt blends with *adobe*.

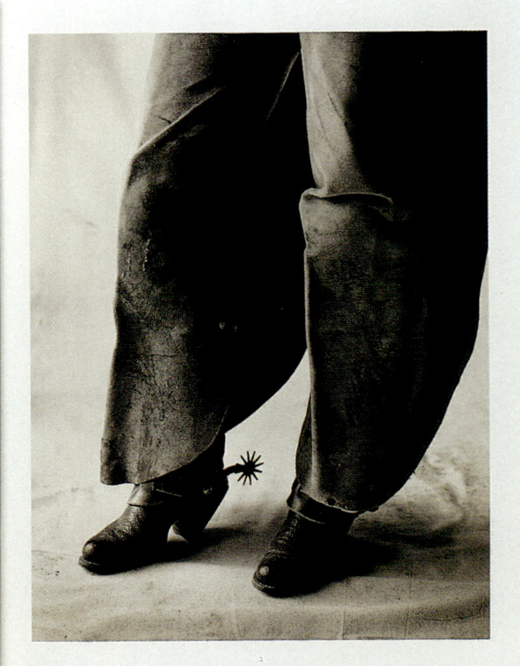

IF YOU LIKE HORSES, cowboying is a good life. Cowboys get to be with horses, even in inclement weather. And horses kick cowboys from time to time, and step on them, and fall on them. Some horses refuse to load in a trailer or let their riders put on a slicker. Horses can be dangerous, beautiful, partners.

(this spread) Design Firm **Rolling Stone Magazine** Art Director and Designer **Fred Woodward** Photographer **Kurt Markus**

MY TROUBLE with cowboys is that their flair for doing the unexpected has infected me, only I lack their improved timing and skill. I suppose I am not alone if I found in them a piece now thought missing in most of mankind, and, after having caught the scent and elusive image of it, wanted to claim it for myself. But I won't give up free-choice coffee and other comparable luxuries, so I'll never win the completeness and the resulting charm women find seductive; women probably see in cowboys figures who can straighten out other messy lives with their black-and-white wills of hard living. It seems that way with cowboys, given their ease in big country and small bars and how they either make things happen or not happen.

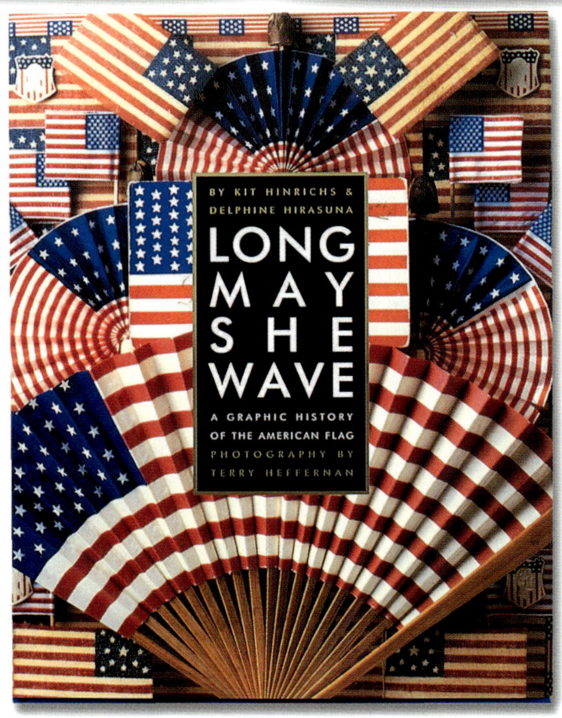

(this spread) Design Firm **Pentagram Design** Creative Director **Kit Hinrichs** Designers **Kit Hinrichs, Shelby Carr** and **Takayo Muroga** Photographer **Terry Heffernan** Copywriters **Delphine Hirasuna, Kit Hinrichs** and **Gerard C. Wertkin**

Toy Biplane
Circa 1920
Japan
Printed Tin
5" x 2.5" x 2.25"
World War I
Replica Model Airplane
Circa 1990
USA
Painted Plastic
5" x 16" x 12.25"
This replica of a World
War I biplane is part
of a series of collectible
American airplanes
from the period.

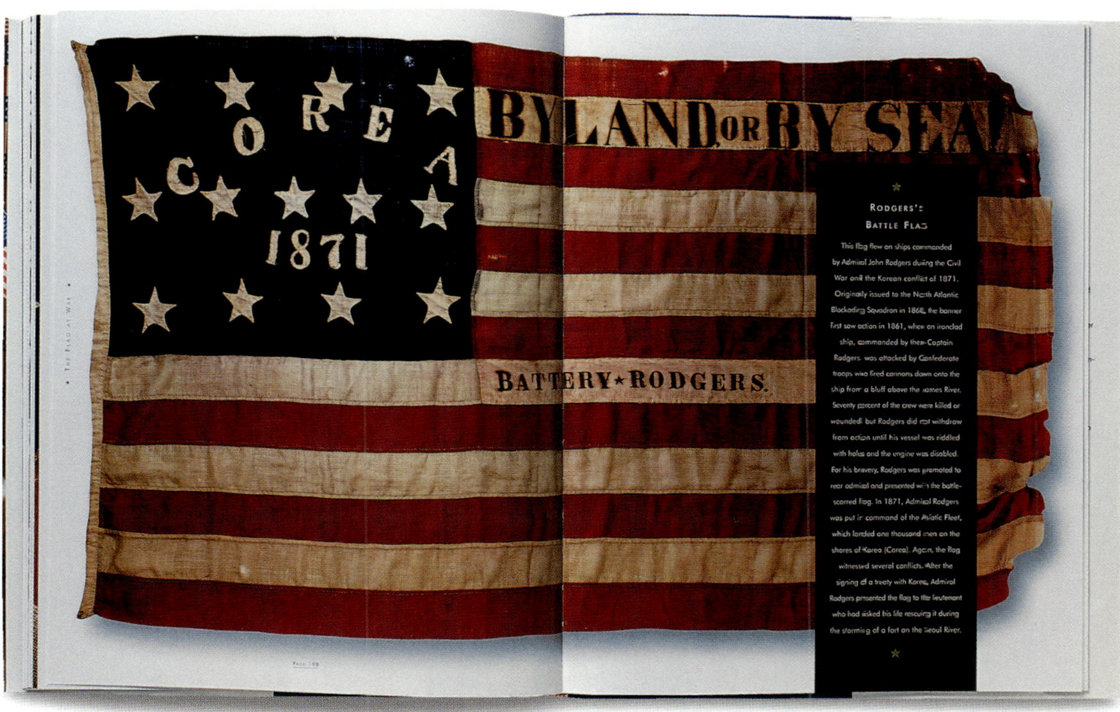
COREA
1871
BY LAND OR BY SEA
BATTERY★RODGERS.
Rodgers's
Battle Flag
This flag flew on ships commanded
by Admiral John Rodgers during the Civil
War and the Korean conflict of 1871.
Originally issued to the North Atlantic
Blockading Squadron in 1861, the banner
first saw action in 1861, when an ironclad
ship, commanded by then-Captain
Rodgers, was attacked by Confederate
troops who fired cannons down onto the
ship from a bluff above the James River.
Seventy percent of the crew were killed or
wounded, but Rodgers did not withdraw
from action until his vessel was riddled
with holes and the engine was disabled.
For his bravery, Rodgers was promoted to
rear admiral and presented with the battle-
scarred flag. In 1871, Admiral Rodgers
was put in command of the Asiatic Fleet,
which landed one thousand men on the
shores of Korea (Corea). Again, the flag
witnessed several conflicts. After the
signing of a treaty with Korea, Admiral
Rodgers presented the flag to the lieutenant
who had risked his life rescuing it during
the storming of a fort on the Seoul River.

CHICAGO
LEADER SPARKLERS
CAUTION FLAMMABLE
U.S. POSTAGE
4c

STATES
PHOTOGRAPHS
RISTOPHER GRIFFITH
ESSAY BY DOUGLAS COUPLAND

U.S. AIR FORCE
554

773B
CAT

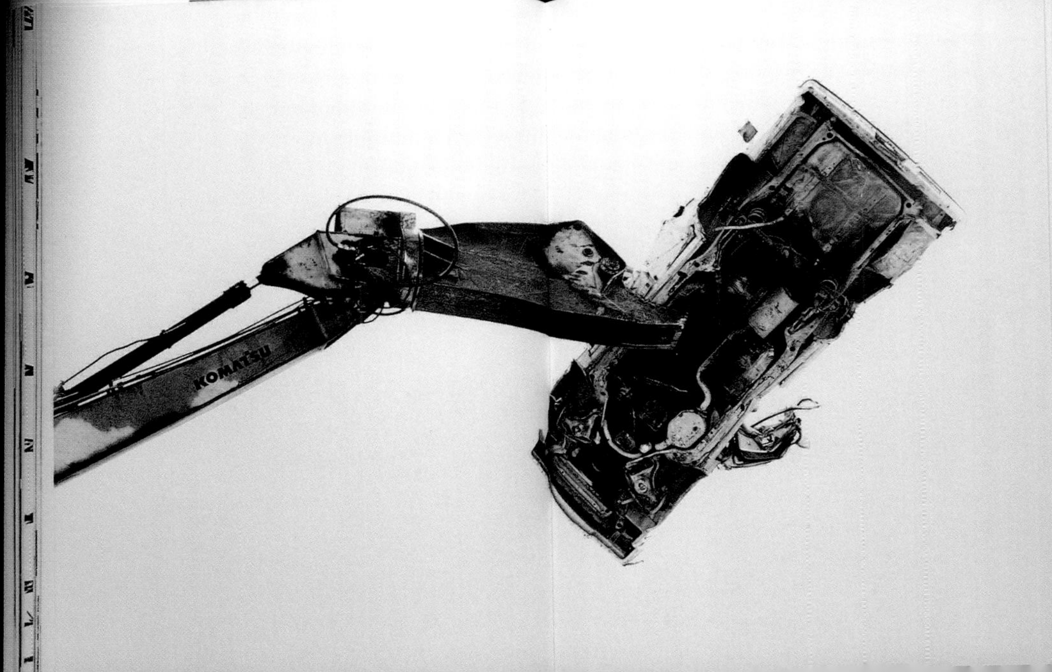
KOMATSU

HELP
ALEXANDER MCQUEEN'S REPLY
TO MY SUGGESTION THAT
SOMETHING BE WRITTEN ACROSS
HIS FOREHEAD.

SHARP
SHARP

27 STALL 1999

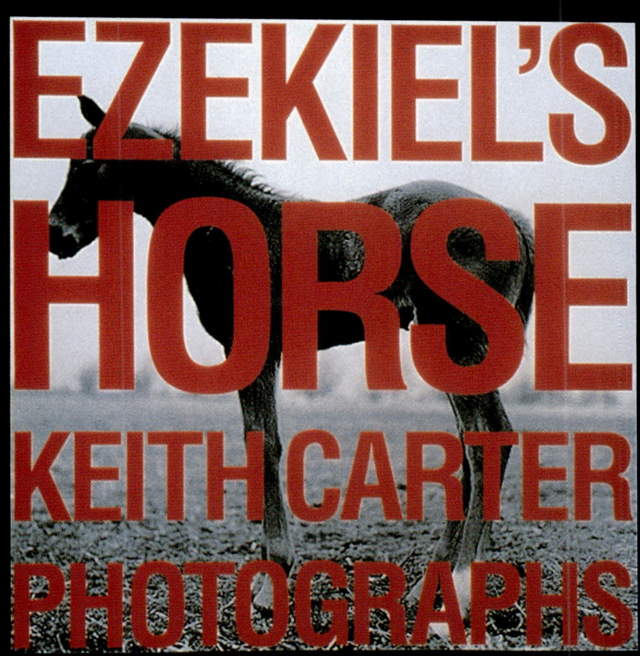

16 RUBENESQUE 1999

Art Director and Designer **Fred Woodward** (Rolling Stone Magazine) Client **American Institute of Graphic Arts**

Design Firm **DNA Design Ltd.** Creative Director, Art Director and Designer **Charlie Ward** Photographer **David Hamilton** Client **Alexandra Von der Beeck**

Design Firm **Drive Communications** Creative Director and Designer **Michael Graziolo** Client **Tor Books**

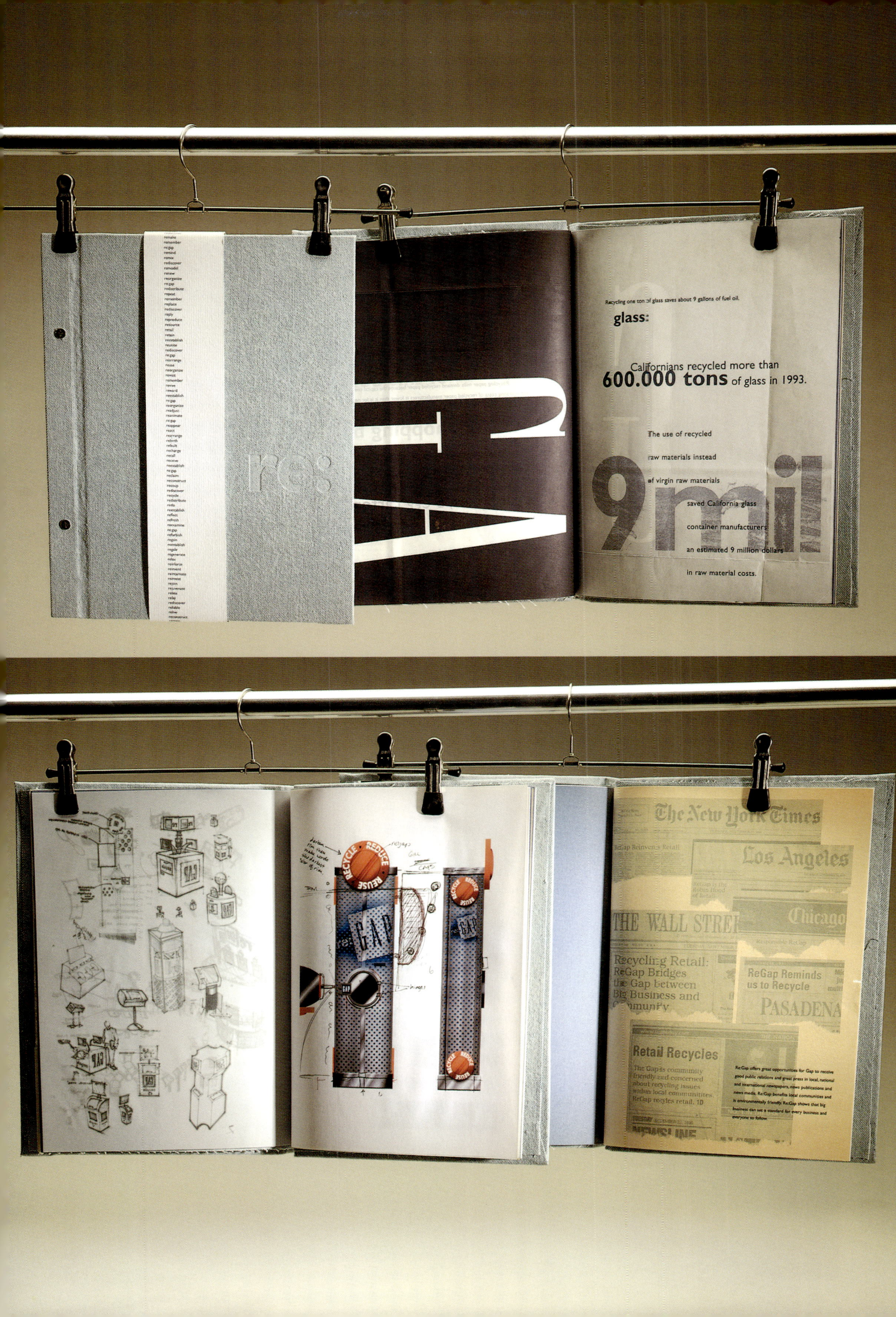

Design Firm **Art Center College of Design** Creative Directors, Art Directors, Designers and Copywriters **Deborah Cook** and **Mirka Meyer** Illustrator **Jason Chatterly** Client **The Gap**

Design Firm **Designframe** Creative Director **Michael McGinn** Art Directors **Michael McGinn, Alexander Polakov** and **Jim Sebastian** Designers **Kazuo Akiyan** and **Alexander Polakov** Photographer **Jim Sebastian** Client **Designtex**

AND HERE'S
YOUR CHANCE TO
WIN THIS
RARE
ROADSTER
AND LOTS OF OTHER
INCREDI-BULL
PRIZES

BY ENTERING THE SWEEPSTAKES
YOU NOT ONLY WILL BE IN THE
RUNNING FOR ONE OF THE
BEEFY CRUISERS, BUT YOU'LL ALSO
HAVE A CHANCE TO WIN
HUNDREDS
OF
INSTANT PRIZES
CD PLAYERS
35MM CAMERAS
CORDLESS PHONES

So be on the lookout for all of our special announcements and promotions.

Design Firm **Henderson Tyner Art Co.** Creative Director **Hayes Henderson** Designer **Andy Trantham** Photographer **Lee Runion** Illustrator **Tim Anderson** Client **Hanes Printables**

In fact, no one at CTD can remember the origins of our name. But we certainly know the values it stands for. We're the printers who talk and listen to our clients, and each other, about achieving the highest quality result possible. We have a record of investment in advanced technology bar none, including the latest computer-to-plate systems. We pay passionate attention to detail at every stage of the printing process, always aiming for a flawless final product.

COMMUN
ICATIO
NMEANS
TALKIN
GTOEAC
HOTHER

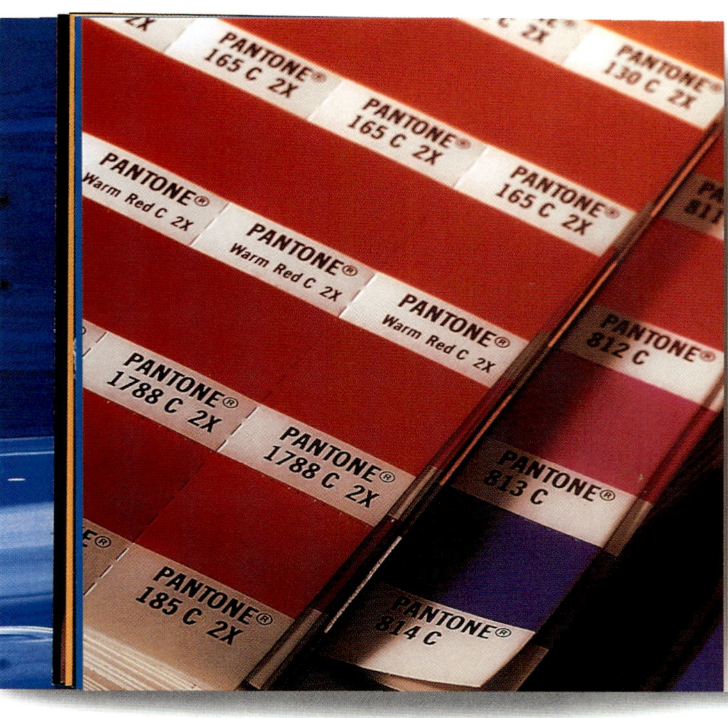

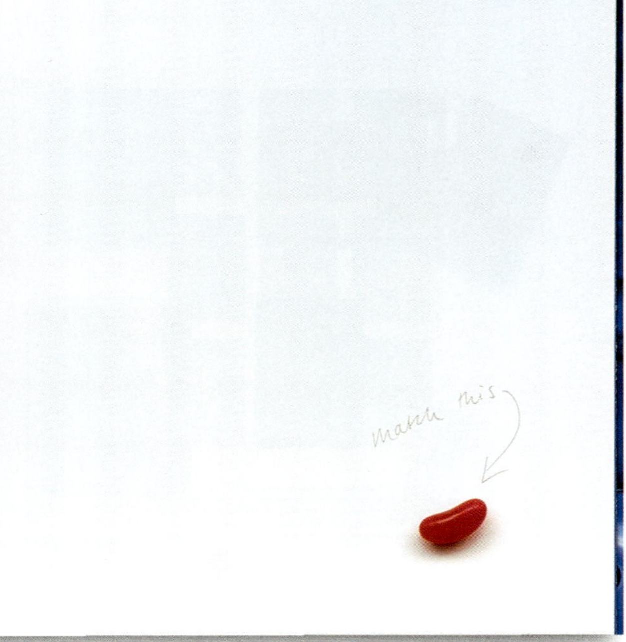

Design Firm **Corporate Edge** Creative and Art Director **Matthew Renton** Designer **Joanne Boswell** Photographers **Matt Cooke** and **Adrian Burke** Copywriter **Pat Smith** Client **CTD Capita**

Design Firm **Henderson Tyner Art Co.** Creative Director **Hayes Henderson** Designers **Christine Celic, Hayes Henderson** and **Elliot Strunk** Photographer **Lon Murdich** Copywriter **Steven Young** Client **Hanes Printables**

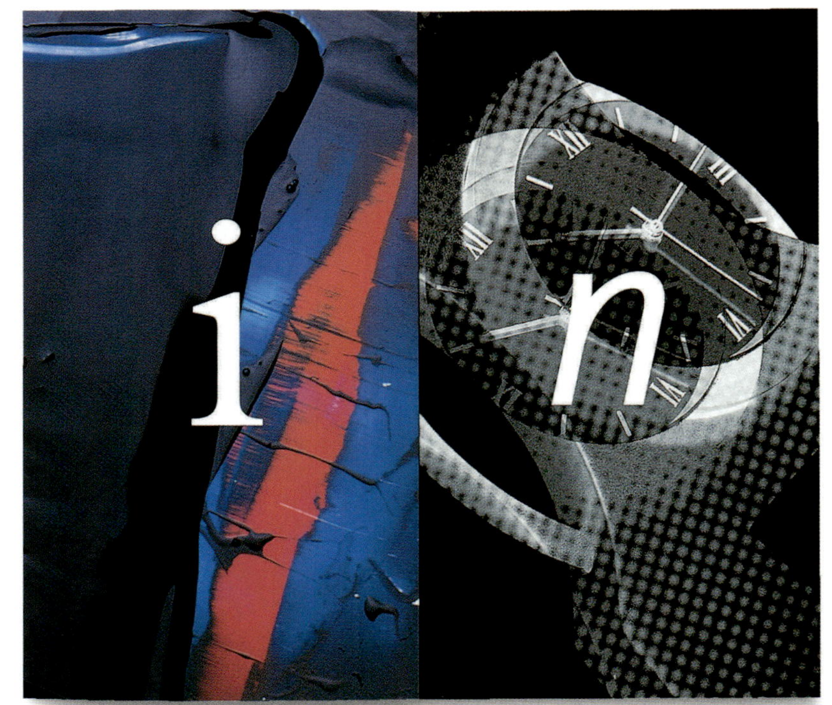

Design Firm **Weymouth Design** Art Director **Tom Laidlaw** Designer **Jonathan Grove** Photographers **Michael Weymouth** and **Michael Indresano** Client **Mead Corporation**

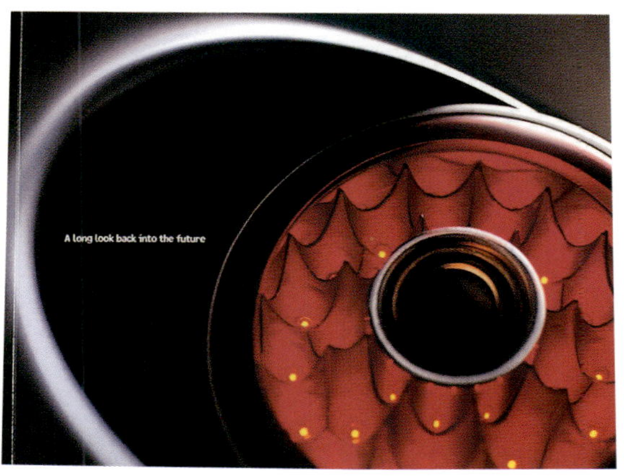

Design Firm **Volcano Design** Creative and Art Director **Tony Donna** Photographer **Harry Vamos** Copywriter **Tony Assenza** Client **Stova/Enzo**

(this spread) Design Firm **Landor Associates** Creative Director **Dennis Merritt** Art Directors **Dennis Merritt** and **Mike Barnett** Designers **Dennis Merritt** and **Craig Arnet** Photographers **Bob Stevens, Brian Trebelcock, Vic Huber** and **Rodney Rascona** Copywriter **John Furr** Client **Lincoln Mercury**

With Navigator, each journey will prove to be an excursion that simultaneously
appeases both your adventurous and sophisticated sides. You pause to reflect
on the day's rewards. So much to be thankful for. So few limitations. Of course,
these revelations are nothing new. They're simply an integral part of every day.

Having found what you came for, it's now time to ponder your next journey. The when's. The where's. But not the how's. That much you know. Thanks to the powerful engine, the excellent handling, and countless amenities within, the answer is clearly Navigator. An assurance of getaways to come.
28
Thanks to the remarkable control of the Lincoln Navigator, you now have the luxury of taking plenty of time to enjoy that which you came for. The fresh air. The breath-taking views. The infinite peace of mind. And, of course, the gnawing desire to experience them once again on your way back home.

08
Lincoln LS in Black Clearcoat. Shown with available equipment.

(this spread) Design Firm **Wood Design** Creative Directors, Designers and Copywriters **Tom Wood** and **Clint Bottoni** Art Director **Tom Wood** Photographer **Craig Cutler** Client **Craig Cutler/Hennegan**

#4.cup 'o joe, black

DINER

din·er
(di'
nər),
n.
1.a person who dines. 2. a small
informal, and usually inexpensive
restaurant.3. a railroad dining
car.4.a restaurant built like
such a car.

Design Firm **M/W** Creative Directors **Allison Williams** and **J. P. Williams** Art Director **Allison Williams** Designers **Allison Williams** and **Yael Eisele** Photographer **Gentl & Hyers** Copywriter **Laura Silverman** Client **Takashimaya New York**

THE SECRET OF LIFE IS REVEALED LITTLE BY LITTLE

Design Firm **Howry Design Associates** Creative and Art Director **Jill Howry** Designer **Todd Richards** Copywriter **Lindsay Beaman** Client **Howry Design Associates**

Bu kitapçığı, kendileri için yaptığımız çalışmaların damağımızda hoş bir tat bırakmasına en az bizim kadar özen gösteren harika reklamverenlerimize ithaf ediyoruz.

movidaplusmap
INTERNATIONAL NETWORK / TANITIM HIZMETLERI A.S.

Design Firm **Movida Plus Map** Creative Director **Oguzhan Akay** Art Director and Designer **Nejat Emrah Yörük** Photographer **Tamer Yilmaz** Copywriter **Yigit Köseoglu** Client **Movida Plus Map**

Design Firm **Shinnoske Inc.** Creative Directors **Tetsuo Kuwano** and **Masaaki Kato** Art Directors **Shinnoske Sugisaki** and **Kenji Fukui** Designers **Shinnoske Sugisaki, Yukichi Takada, Shinsuke Suzuki** and **Makoto Fujita** Illustrators **Yukichi Takada, Seiji Minato** and **Shinsuke Suzuki** Client **Osaka 2008 Olympic Bid Committee**

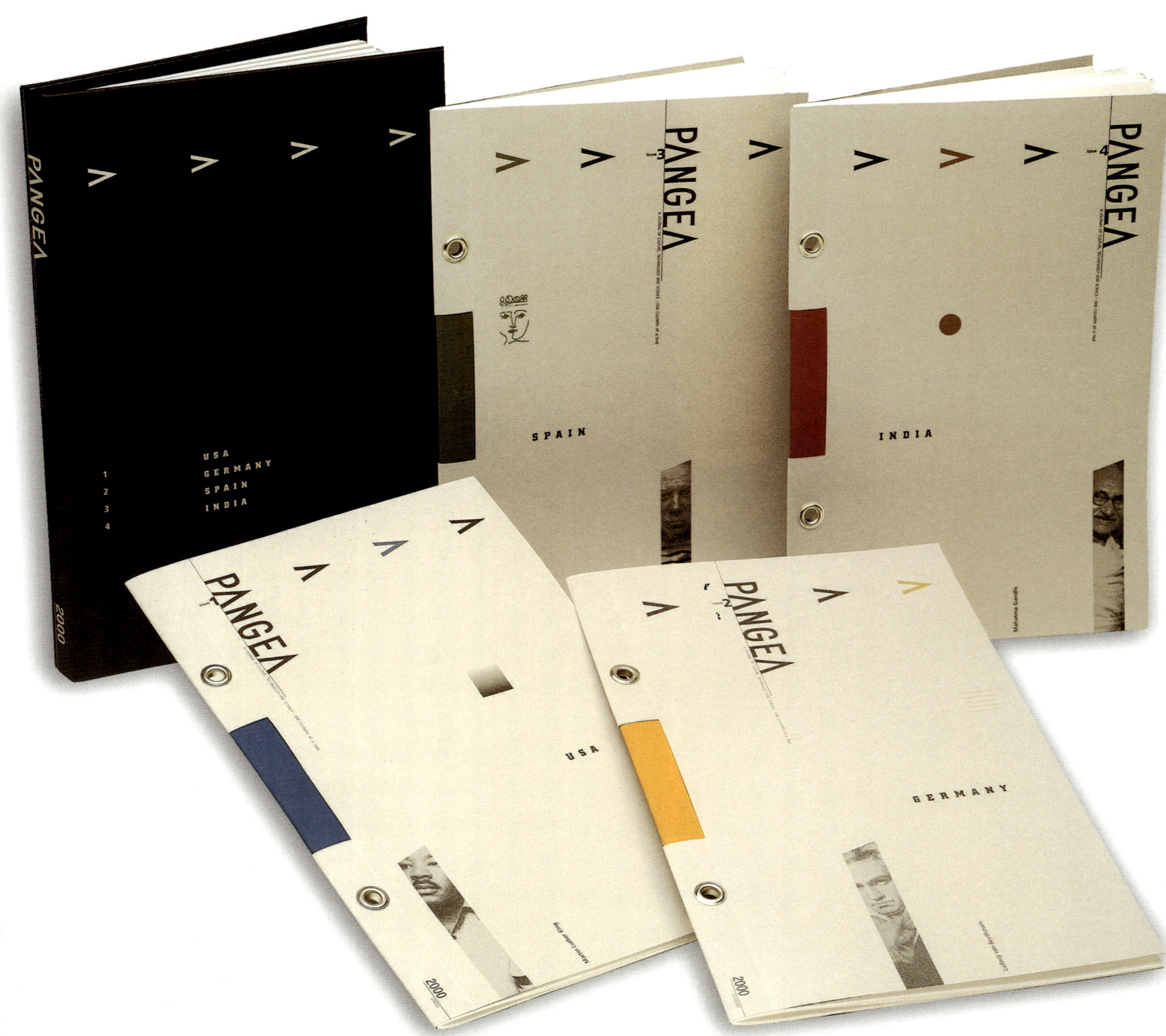

Design Firm **M:C Design Phx:Ffm** Creative Director, Art Director, Designer and Copywriter **Mirka Meyer** Client **Pangea**

"We have to figure out a way to make the training work for everyone, not just people who are comfortable working in front of a computer.

It has to make sense and not scare our people in the field – we call them the 'guys with fat fingers' – who think of a wrench as their only business tool."

EMBRACE IT. USE IT. MASTER IT. DACG

"We never considered ourselves a 'technology' company. These ERP systems have made every company a technology company."

(this spread) Design Firm **Rutka Weadock Design** Creative Director **Anthony Rutka** Designers **Kelda Jackson** and **Anthony Rutka** Copywriters **Kim Carlin** and **Joan Weaver** Client **Maryland Institute, College of Art**

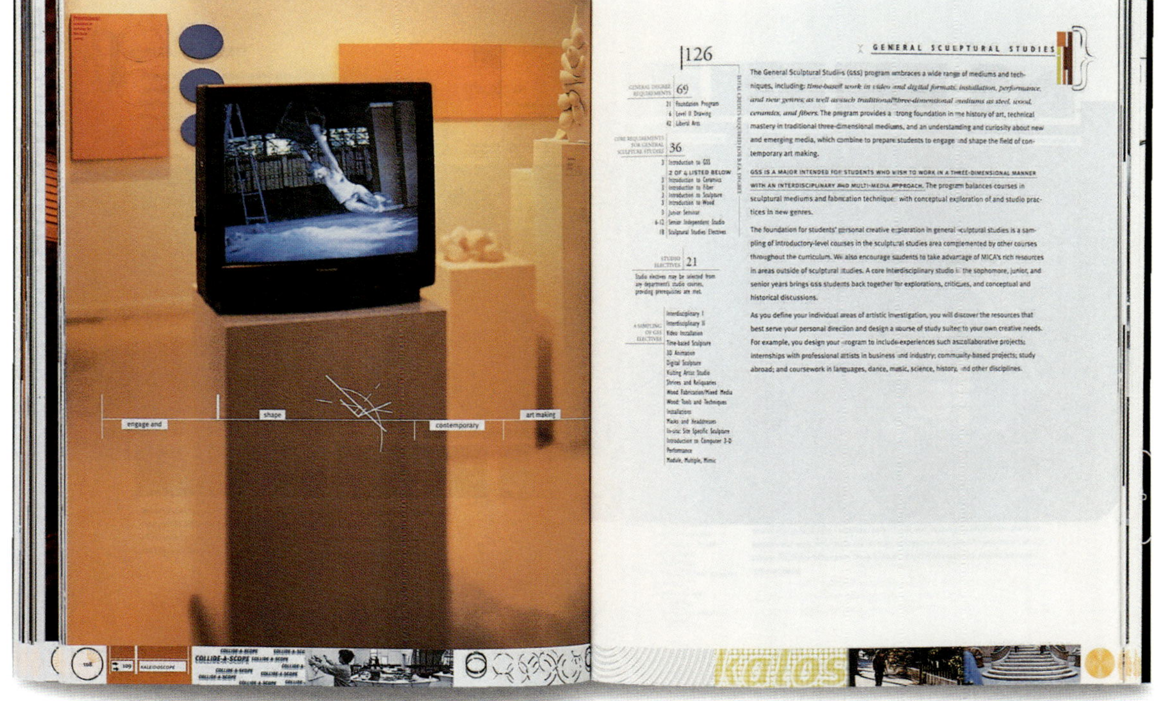

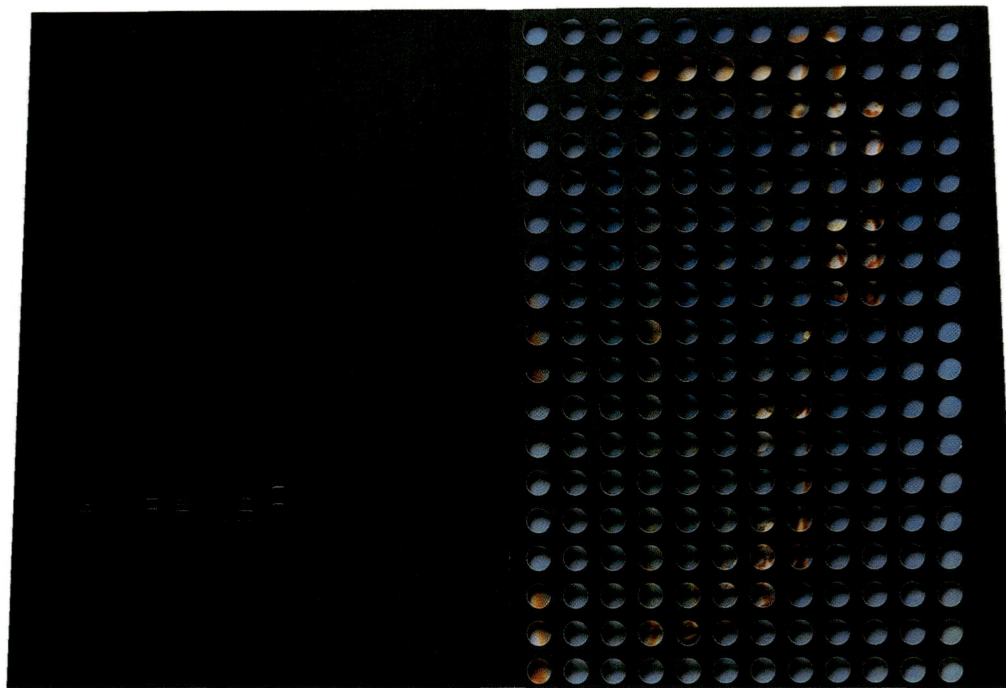

(this spread) Design Firm **advertising, art & ideas ltd.** Creative Director **Stefan Winzeuried** Art Directors and Designers **Fabienne Suter** and **Stefan Winzeuried** Photographer **Ruedi Bosshart** Copywriter **Doris Hofer** Client **advertising, art & ideas ltd.**

PHILIPS

Commercials and advertisement
will bespangle their pictures
with the name, age and profession
of the model shown. Creative
directors want to gain our
confidence in a product by
showing us goodlooking people
who appear so incredibly young.
And as we can see, they aren't!
Feminine models stay extremely
slim, but tough characters
are in demand. That's why
even older woman can model –
as long as they look young.
Male models have to work
out again. A perfect face is
considered boring, a blemish sexy.

2 M	0 M	0 I	1 1	2	3	4	5	6		8	9	10	11	12	13
	15	16	17	18	19	20		22	23	24	25	26	27		29
30	31	1 2	2	3		5	6	7	8	9	10		12	13	14
15	16	17		19	20	21	22	23	24		26	27	28	1 3	2
3		5	6	7	8	9	10		12	13	14	15	16	17	
19	20	21	22	23	24		26	27	28	29	30	31		2 4	3
4	5	6	7		9	10	11	12	13	14		16	17	18	19
20	21		23	24	25	26	27	28		30	1 5	2	3	4	5
	7	8	9	10	11	12		14	15	16	17	18	19		21
22	23	24	25	26		28	29	30	31	1 6	2		4	5	6
7	8	9		11	12	13	14	15	16		18	19	20	21	22
23		25	26	27	28	29	30		2 7	3	4	5	6	7	
9	10	11	12	13	14		16	17	18	19	20	21		23	24
25	26	27	28		30	31	1 8	2	3	4		6	7	8	9
10	11		13	14	15	16	17	18		20	21	22	23	24	25
	27	28	29	30	31	1 9		3	4	5	6	7	8		10
11	12	13	14	15		17	18	19	20	21	22		24	25	26
27	28	29		1 10	2	3	4	5	6		8	9	10	11	12
13		15	16	17	18	19	20		22	23	24	25	26	27	
29	30	31	1 11	2	3		5	6	7	8	9	10		12	13
14	15	16	17		19	20	21	22	23	24		26	27	28	29
30	1 12		3	4	5	6	7	8		10	11	12	13	14	15
	17	18	19	20	21	22		24	25	26	27	28	29		31

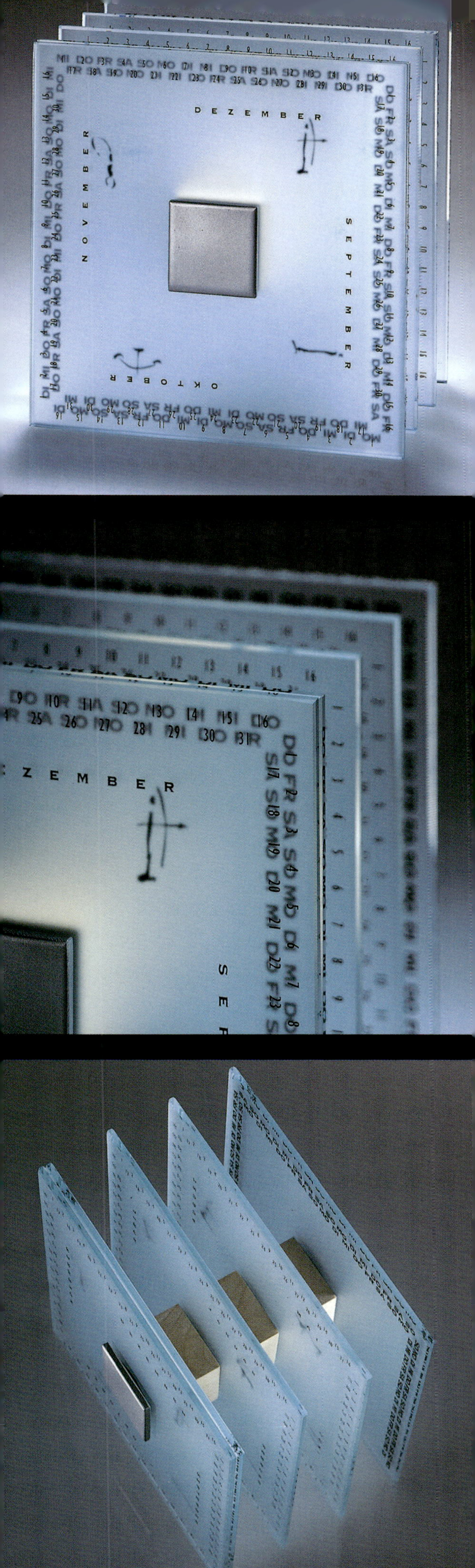
DEZEMBER
NOVEMBER
SEPTEMBER
OKTOBER

Design Firm **Larsen Design & Interactive** Creative Director **Nancy Whittlesey** Designer **Wendy Ruyle** Photographer **Bill Phelps** Copywriters **Rick Emerson** and **Ann Bauleke** Client **Larsen Design & Interactive**

Design Firm **VSA Partners, Inc.** Creative Directors **Ken Fox** and **Mike Petersen** Designer **Adrienne Primosch** Photographer and Illustrator **Harley-Davidson Archives** Copywriter **Jack Sichterman** Client **Harley-Davidson**

Design Firm **Matsumoto Inc.** Creative and Art Director **Takaaki Matsumoto** Designers **Takaaki Matsumoto** and **Larissa Nowicki** Client **Guggenheim Museum**

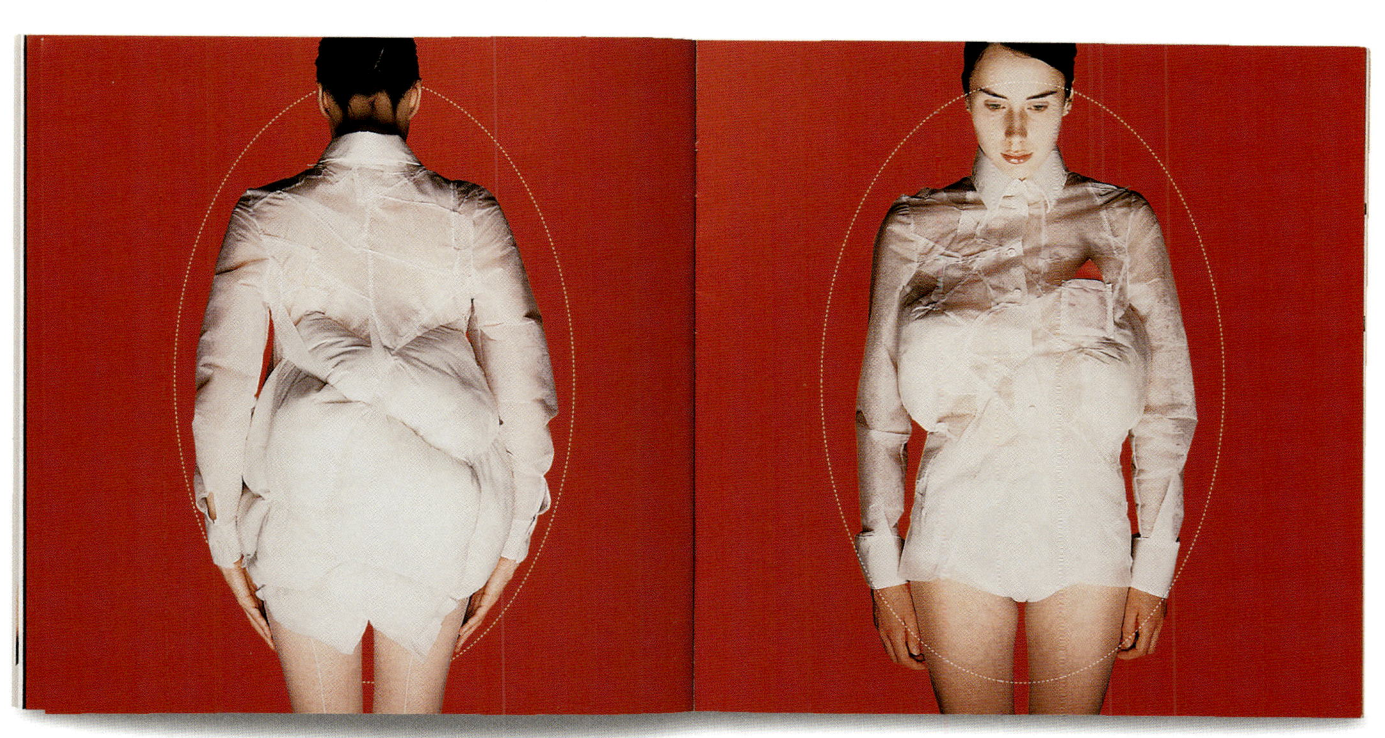

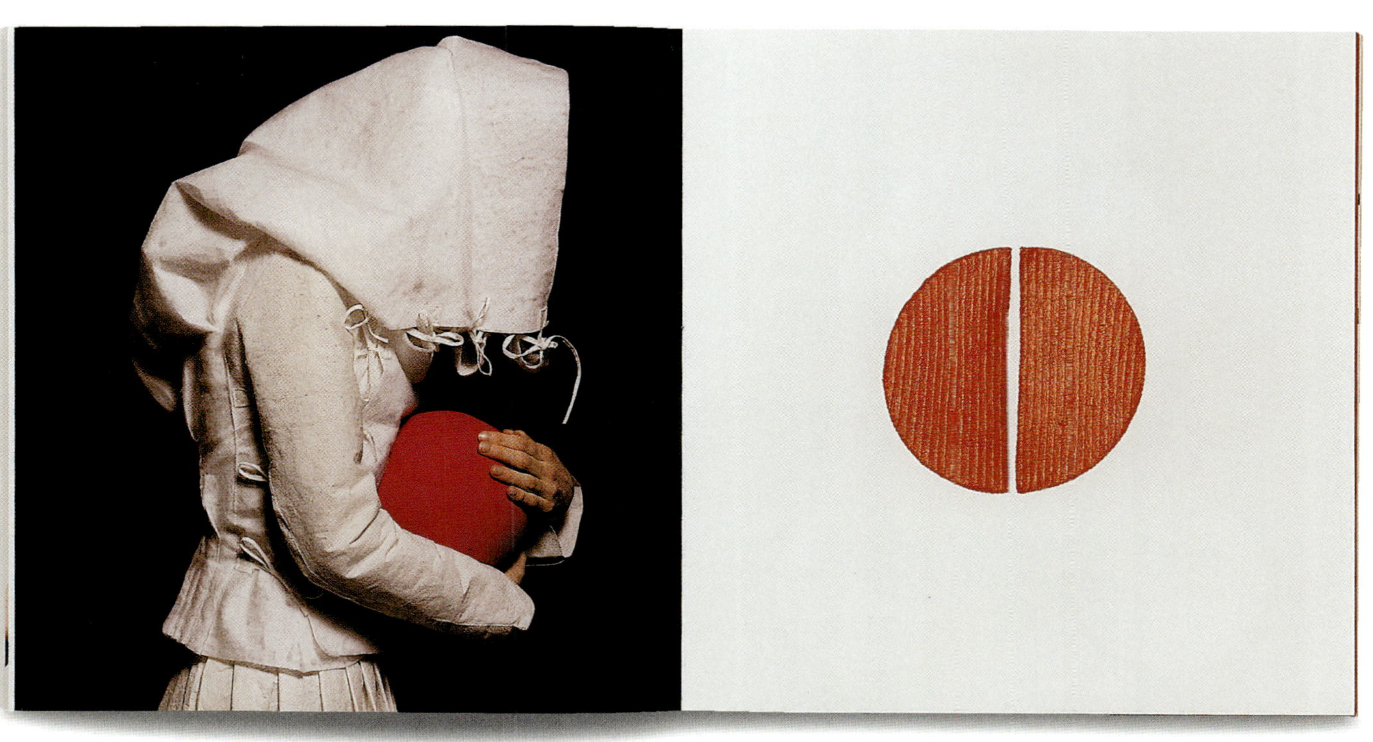

Design Firm **Achtung! Achtung!** Creative Director, Art Director and Designer **Ivana Vucic** Photographer **Vanja Solin** Illustrator **Tomislav J. Kacunic** Client **Textile-Technology Faculty, Zagreb**

Design Firm **Haase & Knels** Creative Director **Sibylle Haase** Art Director and Designer **Katja Hirschfelder** Photographer **Hans Hansen** Client **B. T. Dibbern GmbH & Co. KG**

Design Firm **Heine/Lenz/Zizka** Photographer **Tom Vack** Client **Leica Camera AG**

Design Firm **Seasonal Specialties In-House Design** Art Director **Tracy Olson** Designers **Tracy Olson, Rene Demel, Tricia Sargent, Sharon Wilson, Michelle Scheurer** and **Sean Rage** Client **Seasonal Specialties**

hm29
contract and domestic
seating collection

Hitch Mylius Limited
T +44 (0)20 8443 2616
F +44 (0)20 8443 2617
E info@hitchmylius.co.uk
www.hitchmylius.co.uk

29

hitch|mylius

hm992
design David Chipperfield

Hitch Mylius Limited
T +44 (0)20 8443 2616
F +44 (0)20 8443 2617
E info@hitchmylius.co.uk
www.hitchmylius.co.uk

992

hitch|mylius

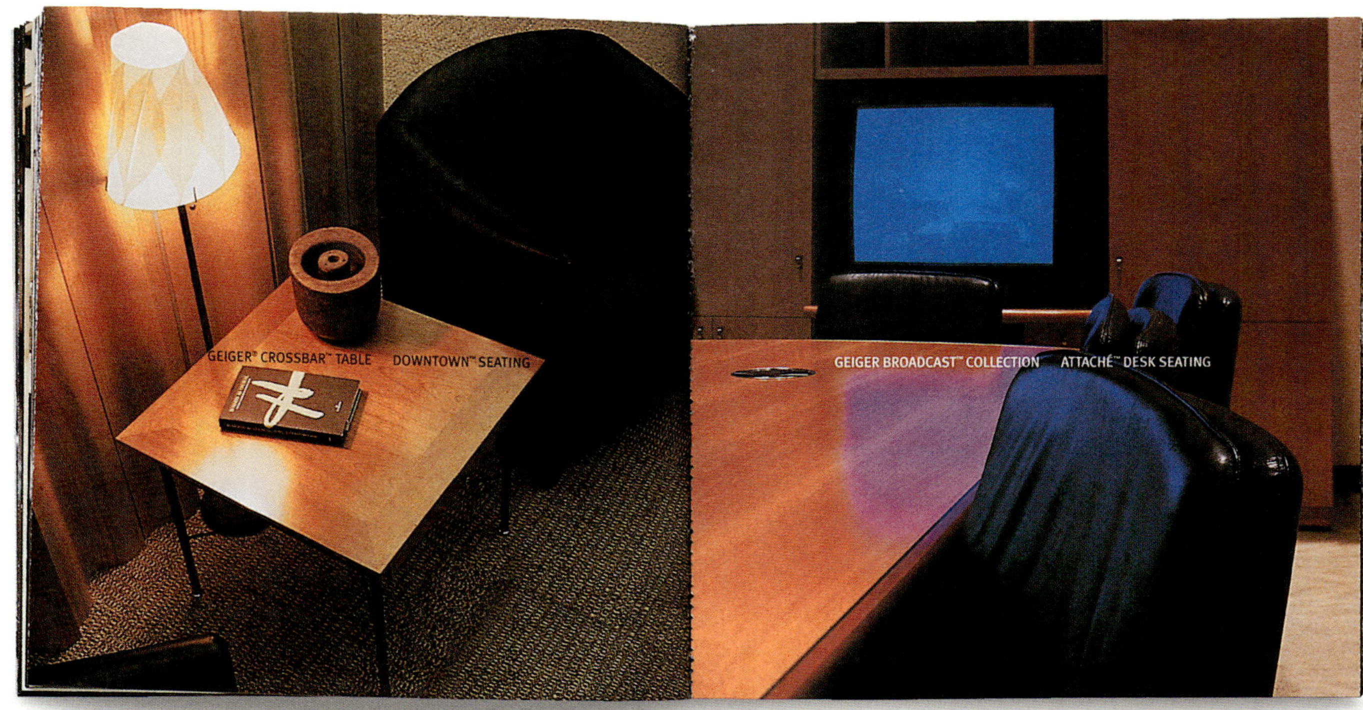

Design Firm **Herman Miller Inc.** Creative and Art Director **Stephen Frykholm** Designer **Brian Edelfson** Photographers **Jim Warych** and **Bill Hebert** Copywriters **Clark Malcolm** and **Dick Holm** Client **Herman Miller Inc.**

MV 1 LOUNGE

MV 10 TABLE

MV 11 TABLES

Design Firm **Vanderbyl Design** Creative and Art Director **Michael Vanderbyl** Designers **Michael Vanderbyl** and **Erica Wilcott** Photographer **Jim Hedrich (Hedrich Blessing)** Client **HBF**

Design Firm **M/W** Creative Directors **Allison Williams** and **J. Phillips Williams** Art Director and Designer **Yael Eisele** Photographer **Ilan Rubin** Client **Sony Style**

Design Firm **Heine/Lenz/Zizka** Client **Messe Frankfurt**

(this spread) Design Firm **HEBE Werbung & Design** Creative Director and Copywriter **Reiner Hebe** Art Directors **Reiner Hebe** and **Katja Maier** Photographers **Niels Schubert, Franics Koenig** and **Dominik Hatt** Client **Maas Goldsmith**

I
l o v e
a l l m y
c l i e n t s
v e r y v e r y
m u c h

Design Firm **TAXI** Creative Director **Jane Hope** Designer **Natalie Cusson** Photographer **Rob Davidson** Copywriter **Peter Ignazi** Client **Virtu**

Design Firm **Ally** Creative and Art Directors **Susanna Cook** and **Emma Oldham** Designer **Soulla Georgiou** Photographers **Diana Miller** and **Tony Torres** Client **Space**

Design Firm **Wink** Creative Directors and Designers **Richard Boynton** and **Scott Thares** Photographers **Klaus Thymann, Earl Kendall, John Barber** and **Karl Herber** Copywriter **Scott Jorgensen** Client **Target**

Design Firm **Finn Nygaard Design** Client **Stelton**

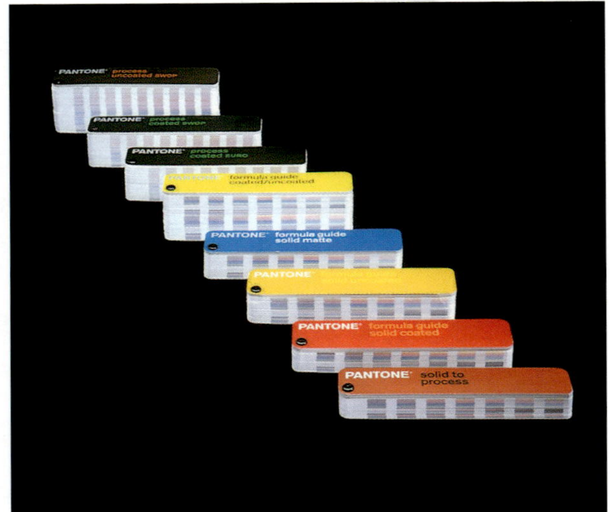

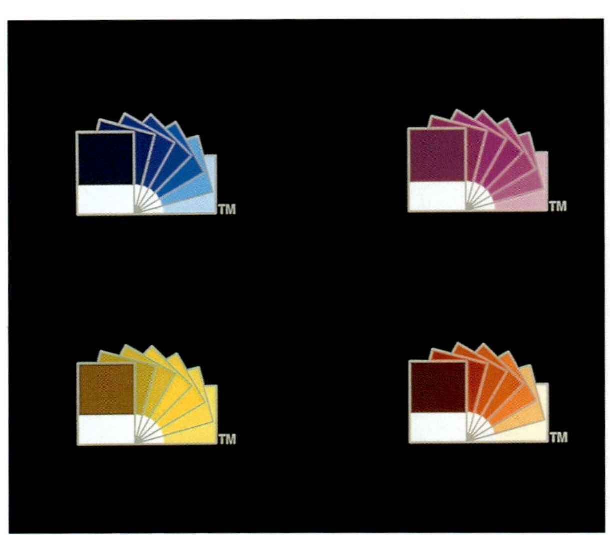

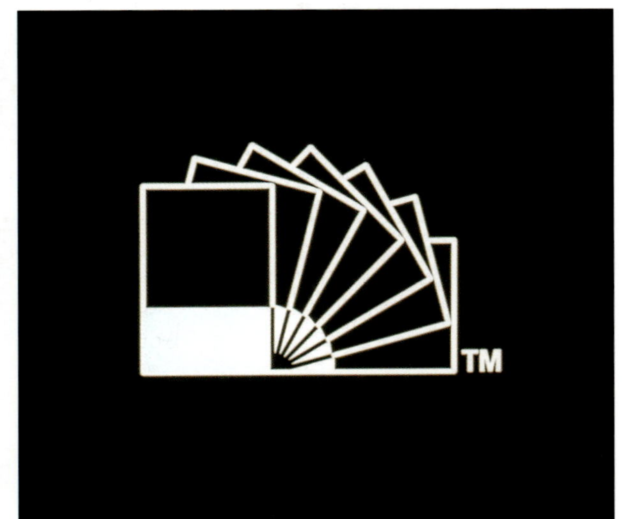

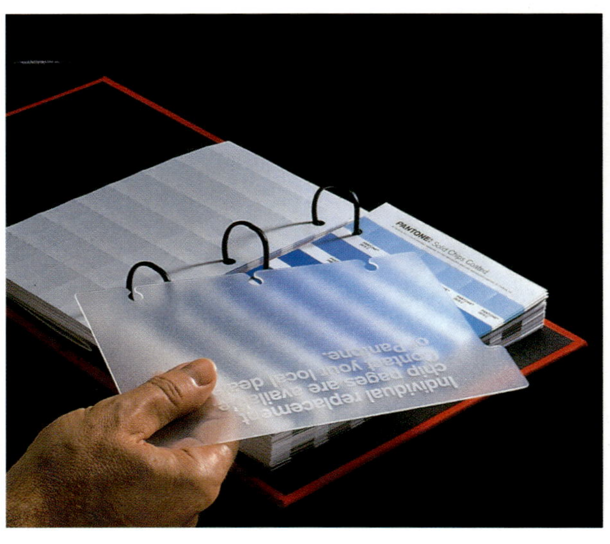

(this spread) Design Firm **Pentagram Design Ltd.** Art Directors **John Rushworth** and **Daniel Weil** Designers **John Dowling** and **Six Wu** Client **Pantone**

SUMA
COCA
MAGDALENA
FLECA
SECALL
XURRO
BRIOIX
GALETA
PANELLET
CANYA
FORN
PA
BARRA
PANETS
CROISSANTS
BAGUETTE
MAGDALENES
ULLERES
PASTÍS
BASTONET
ENSAÏMADES
CROISSANT
PANET
BUNYOLS

770 BROADWAY 770 BROADWAY

ROADWAY

(this spread) Design Firm **Templin Brink Design** Creative Directors **Gaby Brink** and **Joel Templin** Designer **Kris Delaney** Illustrator **Richard Borge** Copywriter **Lessley Berry** Client **Quiver Inc.**

THE QUIVER SOLUTION
HOW DOES IT WORK?
Quiver's proprietary client/server technology captures your users' preferences based on the URLs they contribute, the sites they bookmark, and their clickstream data. Then it automatically builds and continually updates a highly relevant, Community-Powered Directory™ with your brand's look and feel.
GATHER
PROCESS
DELIVER
WANT TO FIND OUT MORE?
CONTACT US FOR MORE INFORMATION ABOUT QUIVER AND OUR COMMUNITY-POWERED™ SEARCH SOLUTIONS.
www.quiver.com
bizdev@quiver.com
415_863_9945
415_863_9946
READY TO GET ON TARGET?
It's easy. We work with you to tailor the initial directory. Then we jointly develop site-integration and marketing plans to ensure a successful launch. All at a substantially lower cost than in-house solutions.
INVOLVING
INTELLIGENT
RELEVANT
SCALABLE

(this spread) Design Firm **Frost Design** Creative and Art Director **Vince Frost** Designers **Vince Frost** and **Melanie Mues** Client **D&AD**

&9
AMPERSAND ISSUE 9 AUGUST – OCTOBER 2000

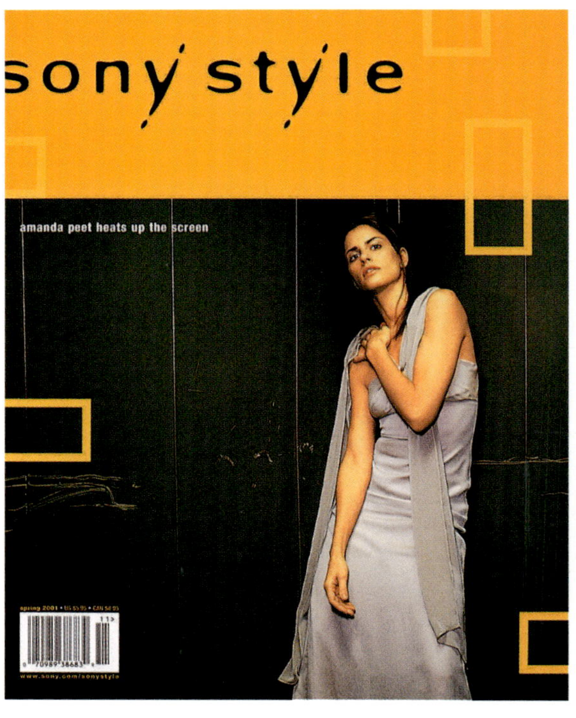

(this page, left) Design Firm **Time Inc. Custom Publishing** Creative Director **Terry Koppel** Art Director **Jennifer S. Muller** Designers **Jennifer S. Muller** and **Min Hee Park** Photographer **Kwaku Alston** Client **Sony Electronics** (right) Design Firm **Time Inc. Custom Publishing** Creative Director **Terry Koppel** Art Director and Designer **Jennifer S. Muller** Photographer **Marc Baptiste** Client **Sony Electronics** (opposite, from top) (**1**) Design Firm **Time Inc. Custom Publishing** Creative Director **Terry Koppel** Art Director and Designer **Jennifer S. Muller** Photographer **Richard Ballard** Client **Sony Electronics** (**2**) Design Firm **Time Inc. Custom Publishing** Creative Director **Terry Koppel** Art Director **Jennifer S. Muller** Designers **Terry Koppel** and **Jennifer S. Muller** Photographer **Marc Baptiste** Client **Sony Electronics** (**3**) Design Firm **Time Inc. Custom Publishing** Creative Director **Terry Koppel** Art Director **Jennifer S. Muller** Designers **Terry Koppel** and **Jennifer S. Muller** Photographer **Kwaku Alston** Client **Sony Electronics**

originality | wow
W
O
W
SHARE THE MUSIC
MUSIC, MOVIES, TV AND THE COOLEST NEW ELECTRONIC PRODUCTS ON THE PLANET
sony style

wyclef
jean
THE FREETHINKING HIP-HOP GENIUS SHARES HIS ECLEFTIC WORLDVIEW
By Josh Dean Singer-songwriter Wyclef Jean says he has a billion songs in his head. Which means a lot of albums for himself and the thousand other artists who'd kill to work with him once he's found time. First, he needs time to tout Ecleftic–Two Sides Two a Book (Sony/Columbia), his new album, and finish its companion, which he predicts will be out by year's end. Time to tour the new material, time to produce his brother and sister's band, Melky Sedeck, or yes, time to regroup with Lauryn Hill and Prakazrel "Pras" Michel for the long, long, long-awaited follow-up to the best-selling rap album of all time, The Score (Ruffhouse/Columbia), which sold 11 million copies on its way to making pop icons of the
PHOTOGRAPHS BY MARC BAPTISTE
sony style FALL 2000

originality | actress

ROBIN
t
TUNNEY
PEAK PERFORMANCE
On a perfectly gorgeous Tuesday morning in August, 28-year-old actress Robin Tunney sits by the window of a small French bistro in downtown Manhattan, the sunlight bouncing off her face with photographic precision. It makes her glow as she leans back, wearing a white blouse styled in that messy-deliberateness. Her eyes are wide and shining. It's a cool, serene image, the perfect picture of a rising star—the good witch from The Craft; the troubled girl with Tourette's syndrome in Niagara, Niagara; the almost-bride of Satan from End of Days; and now, the girl trapped in a cave in the new mountain-climbing blockbuster, Vertical Limit.
Whether she's escaping from the devil in End of Days or dodging avalanches in Vertical Limit, ROBIN TUNNEY never says never. by Ted Gideonse
sony style

(top left) Design Firm **The Observer** Art Director and Designer **Wayne Ford** Photographer **Simon Rawles** Client **The Observer** (top right) Design Firm **The Observer** Art Director and Designer **Wayne Ford** Photographer **Phil Poynter** Client **The Observer**

(bottom left) Design Firm **The Observer** Art Director and Designer **Wayne Ford** Photographer **Harry Borden** Client **The Observer** (bottom right) Design Firm **The Observer** Art Director and Designer **Wayne Ford** Photographer **Patrice de Villiers** Client **The Observer**

(left) Design Firm **The Observer** Art Director and Designer **Wayne Ford** Photographer **Gaultier Deblonde** Client **The Observer** (right) Design Firm **The Observer** Art Director and Designer **Wayne Ford** Photographer **Nick Knight** Client **The Observer**

VISUAL AND PERFORMING ARTS

VOL 4 : NO 1

2wice

RITES OF SPRING

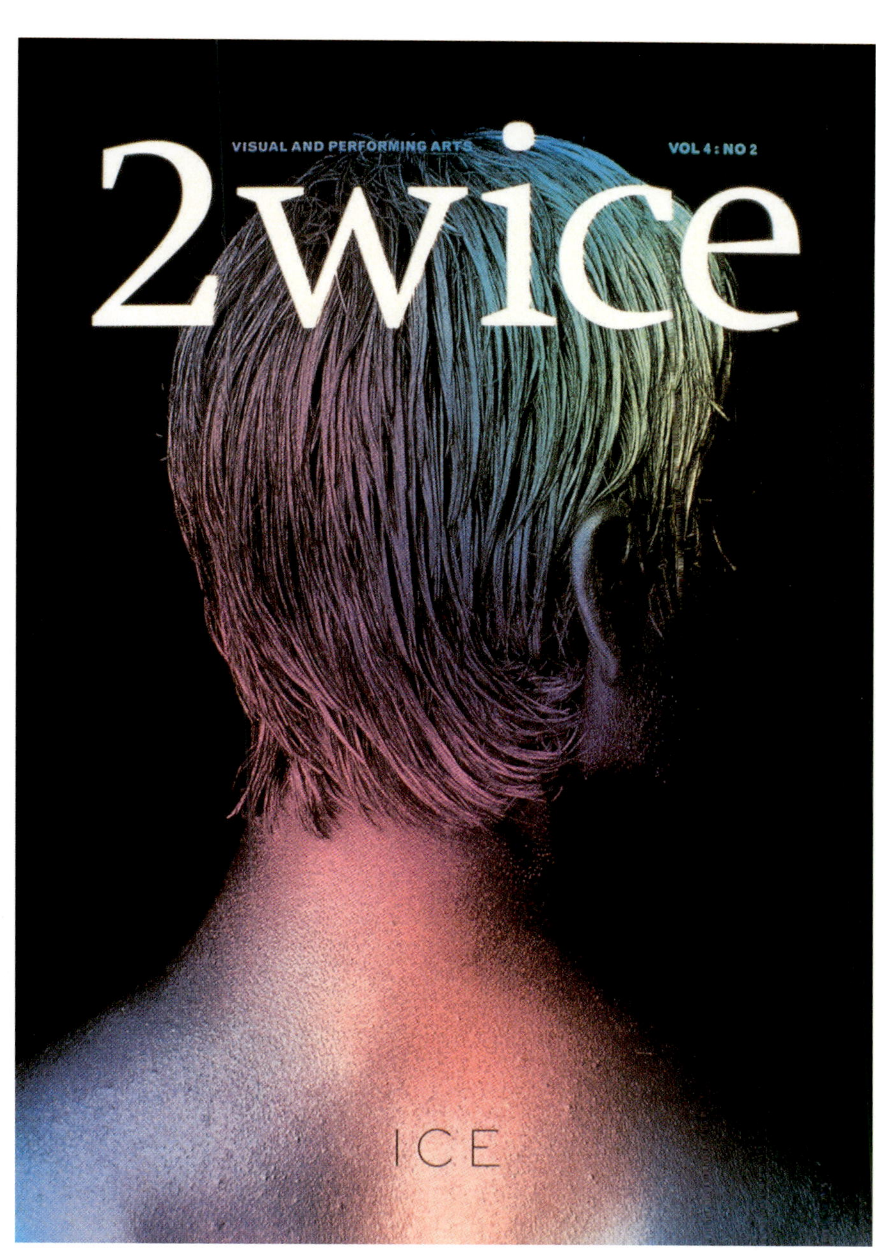
VISUAL AND PERFORMING ARTS
VOL 4 : NO 2
2wice
ICE

Design Firm **Rolling Stone Magazine** Art Director **Fred Woodward** Designers **Fred Woodward** and **Ken Delago** (opposite, from top) **(1)** Design Firm **Rolling Stone Magazine** Photo Editor **Rachel Knepfer** Art Director **Fred Woodward** Designers **Fred Woodward** and **Gail Anderson** Photographer **Martin Schoeller** **(2)** Design Firm **Rolling Stone Magazine** Photo Editor **Rachel Knepfer** Art Director **Fred Woodward** Designers **Fred Woodward** and **Siung Tjia** Photographer **Mark Seliger** **(3)** Design Firm **Rolling Stone Magazine** Photo Editor **Rachel Knepfer** Art Director **Fred Woodward** Designer **Siung Tjia** Photographer **David LaChapelle**

Rolling Stone Sports Hall of Fame 2000

Photographs by Mark Seliger

ARE WE NOT MEN?
WE ARE PEPPERS!
PHOTOGRAPHS BY MARTIN SCHOELLER

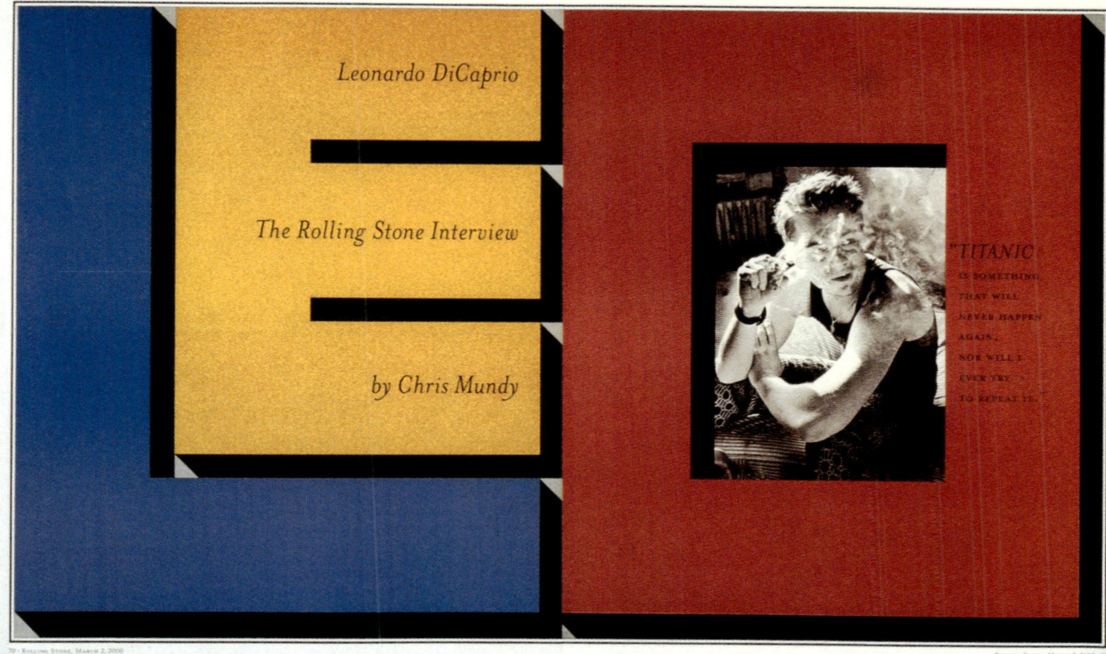
Leonardo DiCaprio
The Rolling Stone Interview
by Chris Mundy
"TITANIC
IS SOMETHING
THAT WILL
NEVER HAPPEN
AGAIN,
NOR WILL I
EVER TRY
TO REPEAT IT."

RECIPE FOR
MARIAH'S LIFE:
MIX ONE PART
SCREWBALL COMEDY,
ONE PART
GLOBAL CAPITALISM.
ADD HIP-HOP
BEATS, SHAKE WELL
IN A PRIVATE
JET AND
SERVE OVER ICE.
BY MIM UDOVITCH
42 · Rolling Stone, February 17, 2000

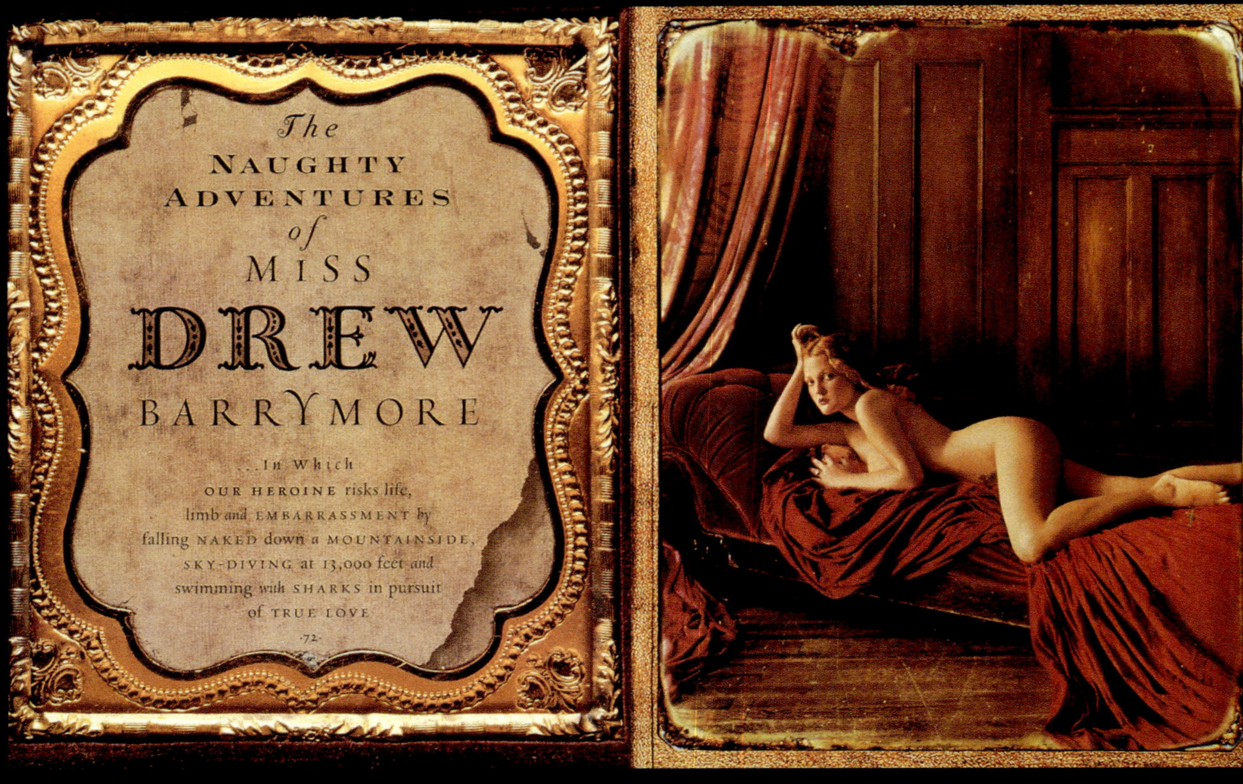

p) Design Firm **Rolling Stone Magazine** Photo Editor **Rachel Knepfer** Art Director **Fred Woodward** Designers **Fred Woodward** and **Lee Berresford** Photographer **Mark Seliger** (bottom) Design Firm **Rolling Stone Magazine** Photo Editor **Rachel Knepfer** Art Director

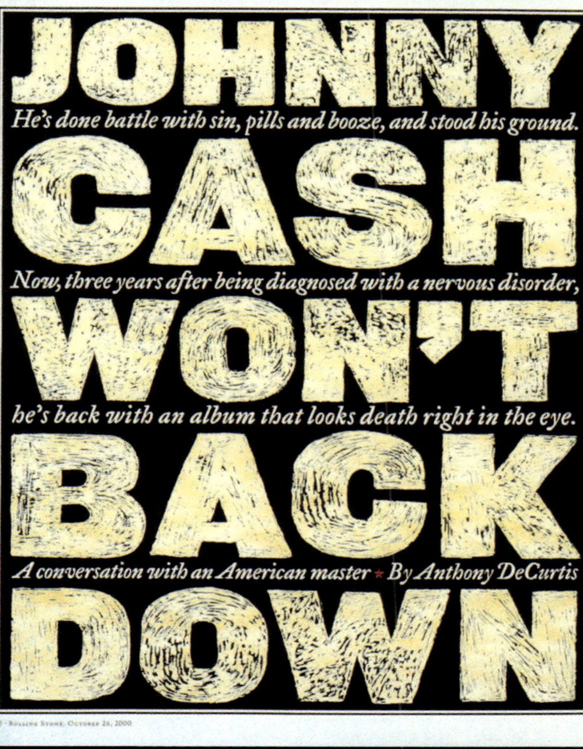

(top) Design Firm **Rolling Stone Magazine** Art Director **Fred Woodward** Designer **Gail Anderson** Illustrator **Bradt Braldts** (bottom) Design Firm **Rolling Stone Magazine** Art Director **Fred Woodward** Designer **Gail Anderson** Illustrator **Alex Ostroy** (from top) **(1)** Design Firm **Rolling Stone Magazine** Photo Editor **Rachel Knepfer** Art Director **Fred Woodward** Designers **Fred Woodward** and **Gail Anderson** Photographer **Mark Seliger** **(2)** Design Firm **Rolling Stone Magazine** Photo Editor **Rachel Knepfer** Art Director **Fred Woodward** Designer **Andy Omel** Photographer **Jean Baptiste Mondino** **(3)** Design Firm **Rolling Stone Magazine** Photo Editor **Rachel Knepfer** Art Director **Fred Woodward** Designer **Ken DeLago** Photographer **William Mercer McLeod**

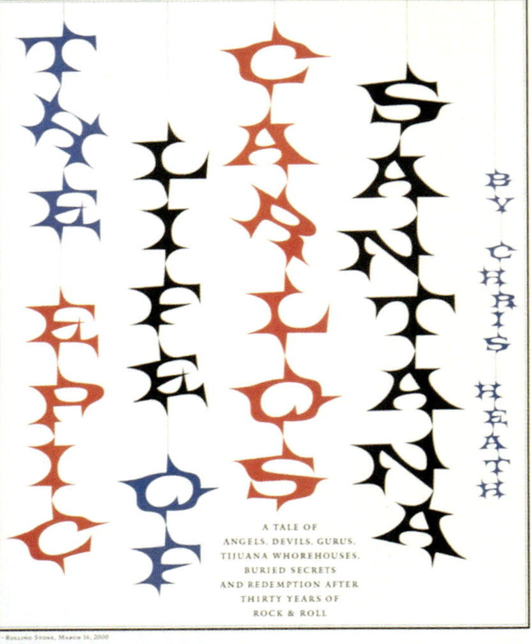

Prisoners of Rock & Roll
Smashing Pumpkins
By David Fricke
Photographs by Jean-Baptiste Mondino

Billy Corgan is sitting in almost total darkness, talking about the end of things. One of them is his interest in writing pop songs. The other is his band, the Smashing Pumpkins.

"I've taken pop songwriting as far as it can go," the singer-guitarist declares. He points at a copy of the band's new

SERENA ★ WILLIAMS

★ ★ ★ TENNIS ★ ★ ★

Design Firm **Exquisite Corporation** Creative Directors **Riley John-donnell** and **Richard Klein** Art Director **Riley John-donnell** Designer **Exquisite Corporation** Photographer **Josh Jordan** Client **Surface Magazine**

Lab
>Arts²
103
Second Nature: Vernis à Ongles nailpolish by **Versace** (Opposite page): Nº 103 Electric by **Shiseido,** Rouge à Levre soft blusher by **Shiseido** Green powder eye shadow by **Nill Color**

Rust velvet & chiffon gown by **Jean-Paul Gaultier** Ornate patterned heavy wrap jacket by **Yohji Yamamoto** White & black embroidered day coat by **Kenzo Homme**

Lab
>Arts³
104
Power Plant: #943 Plum powder blush & #941 Bright pink blush by **Christian Dior** (Opposite page): Bold matte Chrome Yellow eye shadow by **M.A.C.**

top) **(1)** Design Firm **American Airlines Publishing** Art Director **Dianne Gibson** Designer **J. R. Arebalo Jr.** Photographer **Jim Purdum** Copywriter **Chuck Thompson** **(2)** Design Firm **American Way** Creative Director and Designer **Gilberto Mejia** **(3)** Design Firm **American Way** Creative Director **Gilberto Mejia** Designer **Melanie Fowler**

(from top) (**1**) Design Firm **American Way** Creative Director **Gilberto Mejia** Designer **Charles Stone** Photographer **Carl Yarbrough** (**2**) Design Firm **American Way** Creative Director and Designer **Gilberto Mejia** (**3**) Design Firm **American Airlines Publishing** Art Director **Dianne Gibson** Designer **J. R. Arebalo Jr.** Photographer **Grant Kessler** Copywriter **John Mariani** Client **Southwest Airlines**

Sea foam crinkle camisole, Comrags; Green lace wrap skirt, Free People; Yellow glass expandable choker, Dryberg Kern. opposite: Yellow silk skirt with beaded fringe, Reversible silk shawl with vine embroidery, both Easel; Slides, DKNY.

Lemon and lime bias cut dress, Comrags. opposite: Green dress with yellow feathers, David Dixon.

Makeup & Hair: Alex Borovoy, Plutino Group
Stylist: Meileen, Plutino Group
Model: Kari, Ford Models

Chartreuse shell and green crinkle skirt, both David Dixon; Lemon elastic necklace and leather bracelet, Dryberg Kern; Blue feather slides, DKNY. opposite: Periwinkle crinkle dress, handball by Shelli Orr; Frosted glass bead necklace, Memento.

(this page) Design Firm **Fast Company** Creative and Art Director **Patrick Mitchell** Designer **Emily Crawford**

Firm **Pentagram Design** Art Director **Paula Scher** Designers **Paula Scher, Dok Chon** and **Rion Byrd** Photographer **Peter Mauss** Client **New Jersey Performing Arts Center**

(this spread) Design Firm **Skidmore Owings & Merrill LLP** Art Director **Lonny Israel** Designers **Erin O'Reilly, Brad Thomas** and **Matthew Fadness** Photographers **Tim Hursley** and **Lara Swimmer** Client **Experience Music Project**

(this spread) Design Firm **Pentagram Design** Art Director **Paula Scher** Designers **Paula Scher, Dok Chon** and **Rion Byrd** Photographer **Peter Mauss** Client **New 42nd Street Development**

NEW
42
ST
STUDIOS
THE
DUKE
ON 42ND ST
ROUNDABOUT
merica
229

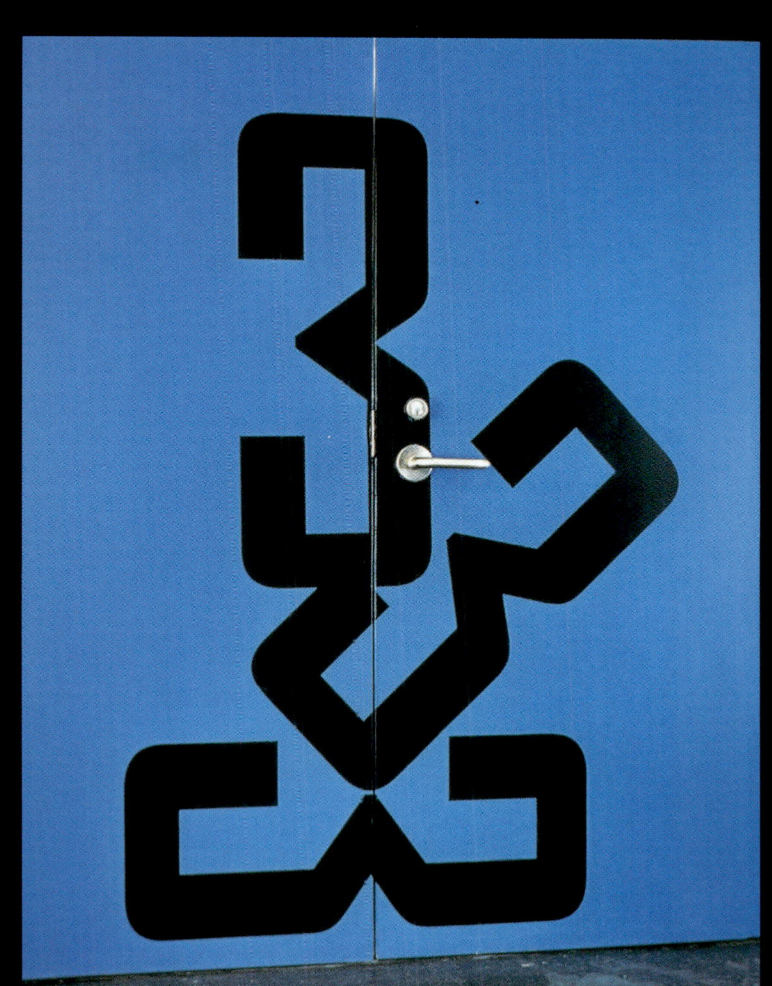

DRESSING ROOMS

10
NEW 42ND ST. INC.
2M
DRESSING ROOMS
PRODUCTION
9
MARIAN HEISKELL
STUDIO 9A
JOAN AND JOE CULLMAN
STUDIO 9B
STUDIO 9C
LuESTHER MERTZ
BOARD RM
6
JERRY ZAKS
STUDIO 6C
STUDIO 6B
STUDIO 6A
1
MARIAN'S LOBBY
8
DRESSING ROOMS
WILLIAMSTOWN THEATRE FESTIVAL
ROUNDABOUT THEATRE COMPANY
PARSONS DANCE FOUNDATION
ADDITIONAL TENANT
4
STUDIO 4A
STUDIO 4B
STUDIO 4C
2
THE DUKE ON 42ND STREET
BOX OFFICE
3
STUDIO 3A
STUDIO 3B
5
BUILDING ADMIN
DRESSING ROOMS
NEW PROFESSIONAL THEATRE
7
JEROME ROBBINS
STUDIO 7A
STUDIO 7B
DOROTHY AND LEWIS B. CULLMAN
STUDIO 7C

(this spread) Design Firm **McMillan Group Inc.** Creative Director **Charlie McMillan** Art Director **Rob Spademan** Designers **Charlie McMillan** and **Nancy McMillan** Project Architect **Structura Architects** Photographer **Jamie Padgett** Client **Marconi Medical Systems**

(top) Design Firm **Pentagram Design** Art Director **Jim Biber** Designers **Michael Zweck-Bronner, Brian Jacobs, Alex Mergold, Andrea Wang, Suzanne Holt** and **Kit Hinrichs** Client **Muzack** (bottom) Design Firm **Pentagram Design** Art Director and Designer **Paula Scher** Client **American Museum of Natural History**

Design Firm **Selbert Perkins Design** Art Director **Robin Perkins** Designers **Nick Groh** and **Clint Woesner** Photographers **Andy Davey** and **Anton Grassl** Client **Los Angeles World Airport**

qiora

(this spread) Design Firm **Shiseido Co. Ltd.** Creative and Art Director **Aoshi Kudo** Designers **Aoshi Kudo** and **Rikiya Uckusa** Photographer **David M. Josepe** Architect **A.R.O., Hiroko Sueyoshi** Client **Shiseido Co. Ltd.**

Design Firm **Origami Communication Design** Creative Director, Art Director, Designer and Illustrator **Michael Wou** Photographer **Ron Levine** Copywriter **Gerry Lipnowski** Clients **Ron Levine** and **Michael Wou**

me
ISSEY MIYAKE

Design Firm **Pentagram Design** Art Director **J. Abbott Miller** Designers **J. Abbott Miller** and **Roy Brooks** Client **Rock & Roll Hall of Fame & Museum**

Design Firm **Pentagram Design** Art Director and Designer **Kit Hinrichs** Exhibition Photographs **Lucca Pioltelli©2000** Client **American Institute of Graphic Arts (AIGA)**

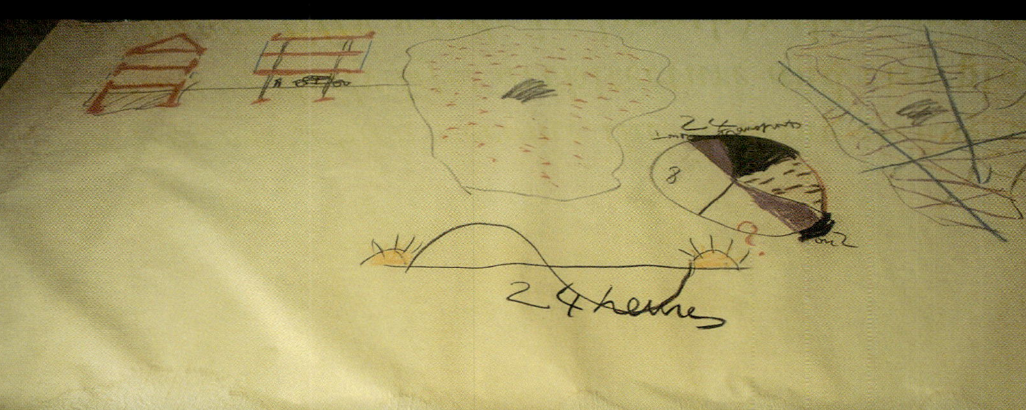

I continue my floors, second, third. And the roof? I don't build one. For the study (and practice) of constructions with central heating in countries of heavy snowfall have shown me that it is better to evacuate melted snow inside a house, where it is warm. (I shall explain later.) My roof will therefore be flat with a slope toward the center of one centimeter per meter, which is imperceptible. But the study of roof terraces in hot countries shows us that the effects of expansion can be disastrous, and provoke cracks through which water will infiltrate. Therefore the roof terrace should be protected from the effect of strong sunshine. For this I create a garden on the roof of my house. These gardens — I have thirteen years of experience in them — in favorable conditions are real hothouses, and trees and plants grow there admirably.

Now I draw the plan, below the two sections; at ground level, the walls of stone of all the centuries before our days and the columns of concrete or iron of the modern house with the ground entirely free.

PRECISIONS

I express the present solar day, as it exists in the USA and in Europe, by a circle.

The first eight-hour sector represents sleep. Tomorrow, and each morning, the day will be new and fresh. [The second sector] *is an hour and a half lost in transportation* — subways, trains, buses, streetcars. [The third sector] *represents today the eight hours of work necessary for production.* [The fourth sector] stands *for time destroyed in transportation. There is a balance* [the fifth sector] *of five leisure hours in the evening: family table, life within the snail shell, the dwelling.*

I draw the vague contour which defines the urban region. In the center is the city — business. Industries, workshops, and factories? They are inside the city or around it, in the stupidity of disorder and shortsightedness. The urban region is an immense reservoir; it contains two, three, five, seven, ten million people! It is twelve, eighteen, thirty, sixty miles in diameter.

WHEN THE CATHEDRALS WERE WHITE

(this spread) Design Firm **Pentagram Design Ltd.** Art Director **Lorenzo Apicella** Client **Natural History Museum U.K.**

(this spread) Design Firm **Pentagram Design** Creative Director **Michael Zweck-Bronner** Art Directors **Jim Biber** and **J. Abbott Miller** Designers **Ivan Arenas, Andrea Wang, James Hicks, Scott Devendorf, Roy Brooks, Elizabeth Glickfeld, John Porter** and **Suzanne Holt** Client **John Bull/Uncle Sam: Four Centuries of British-American Relations**

Design Firm **Murphy Design Inc.** Creative Director, Art Director and Designer **Mark Murphy** Illustrator **Joe Sorren** Client **Joe Sorren**

THE 401(k) COMPANY
GUIDING THE WAY

COSGROVE

Design Firm **Mirko Ilic Corp.** Art Director **Steven Heller** Illustrator **Mirko Ilic** Client **New York Times Book Review**

UNLEADED FUEL ONLY
OCTANE:
FOR OPTIMUM PERFORMANCE
AMOCO
HIGH OCTANE UNLEADED ONLY

S. HENDLER

Design Firm **Rolling Stone Magazine** Art Director **Fred Woodward** Illustrator **Matt Mahurin** Client **Rolling Stone Magazine**

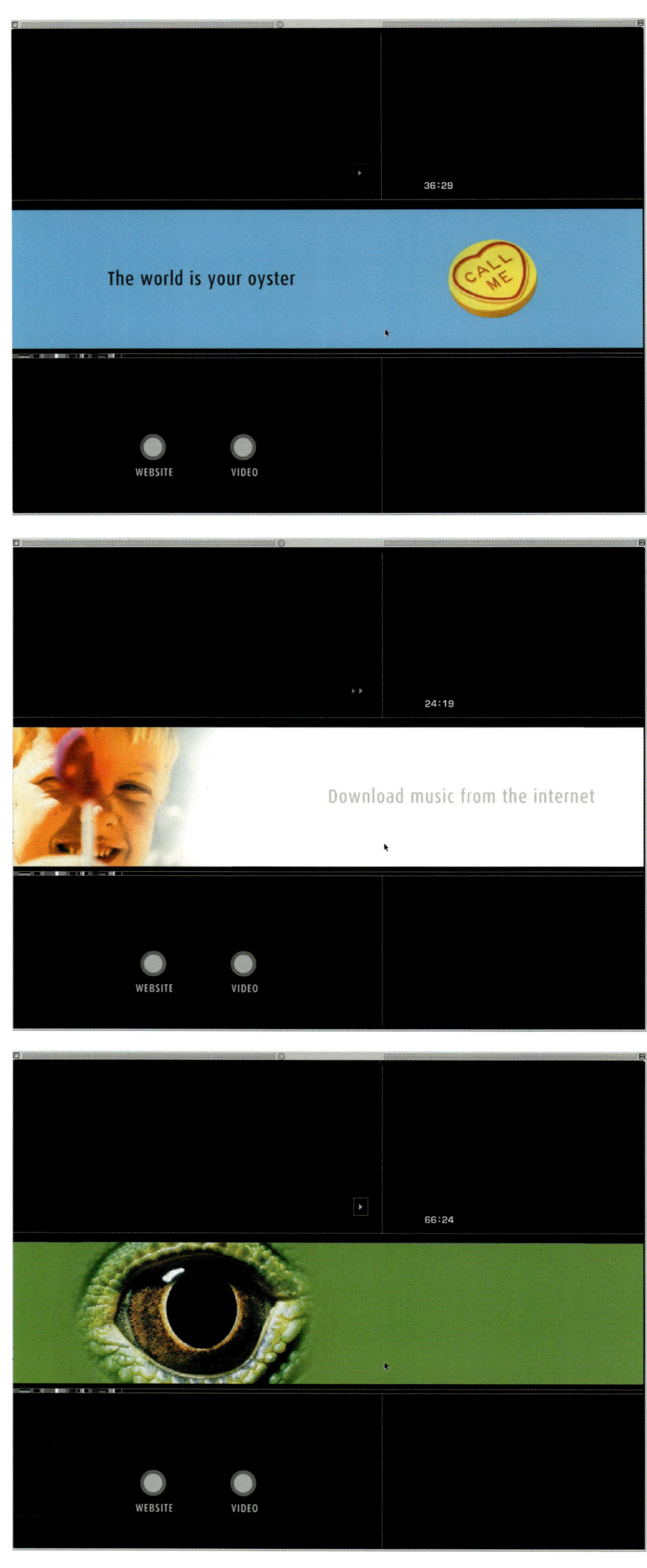

Design Firm **DNA Design Ltd.** Creative and Art Director **Charlie Ward** Designers **Charlie Ward** and **Boy Girl Boy** Copywriter **Andrew Gair** Client **Telecom New Zealand**

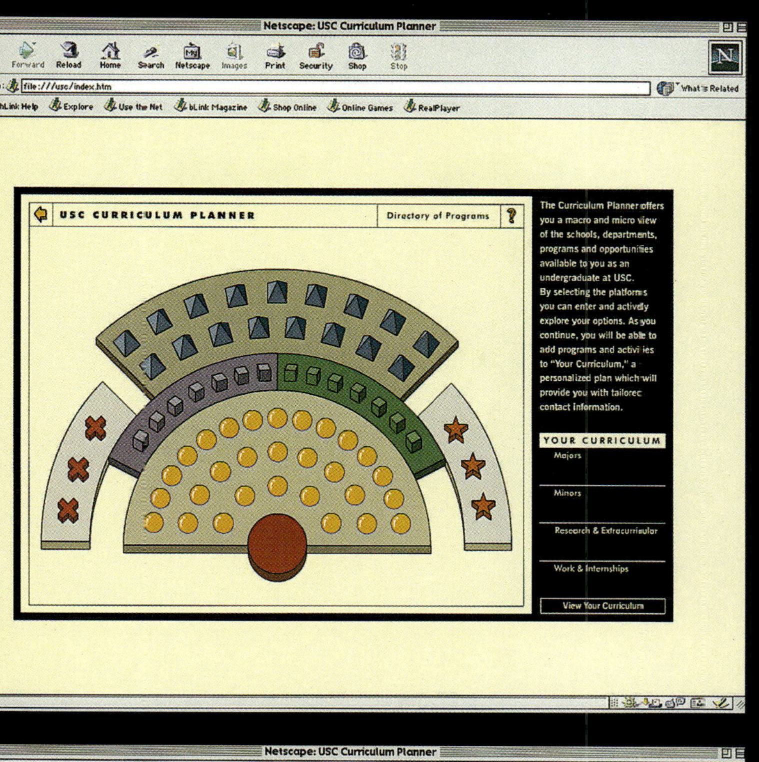

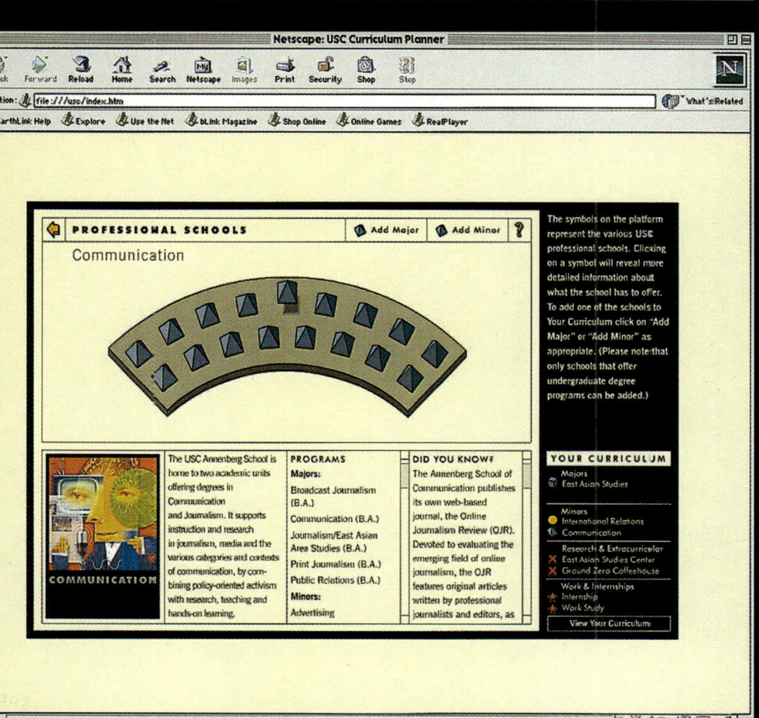

Design Firm **Pentagram Design** Creative Director **Kit Hinrichs** Art Director **Brian Jacobs** Designers **Brian Jacobs** and **Douglas McDonald** Client **University of Southern California**

FIRST AMERICAN MOTORCYCLE
SINCE 1901 CALL 1-800-445-1759
WWW.INDIANMOTORCYCLE.COM
Indian
GROWN MEN HAVE BEEN KNOWN TO WEEP
INDIAN
MAGIC
It's in the blood.
Indian
Since 1901
INDIAN CHIEF Specifications
Contact Us
1-800-445-1759
INDIAN
EST 1 9/01

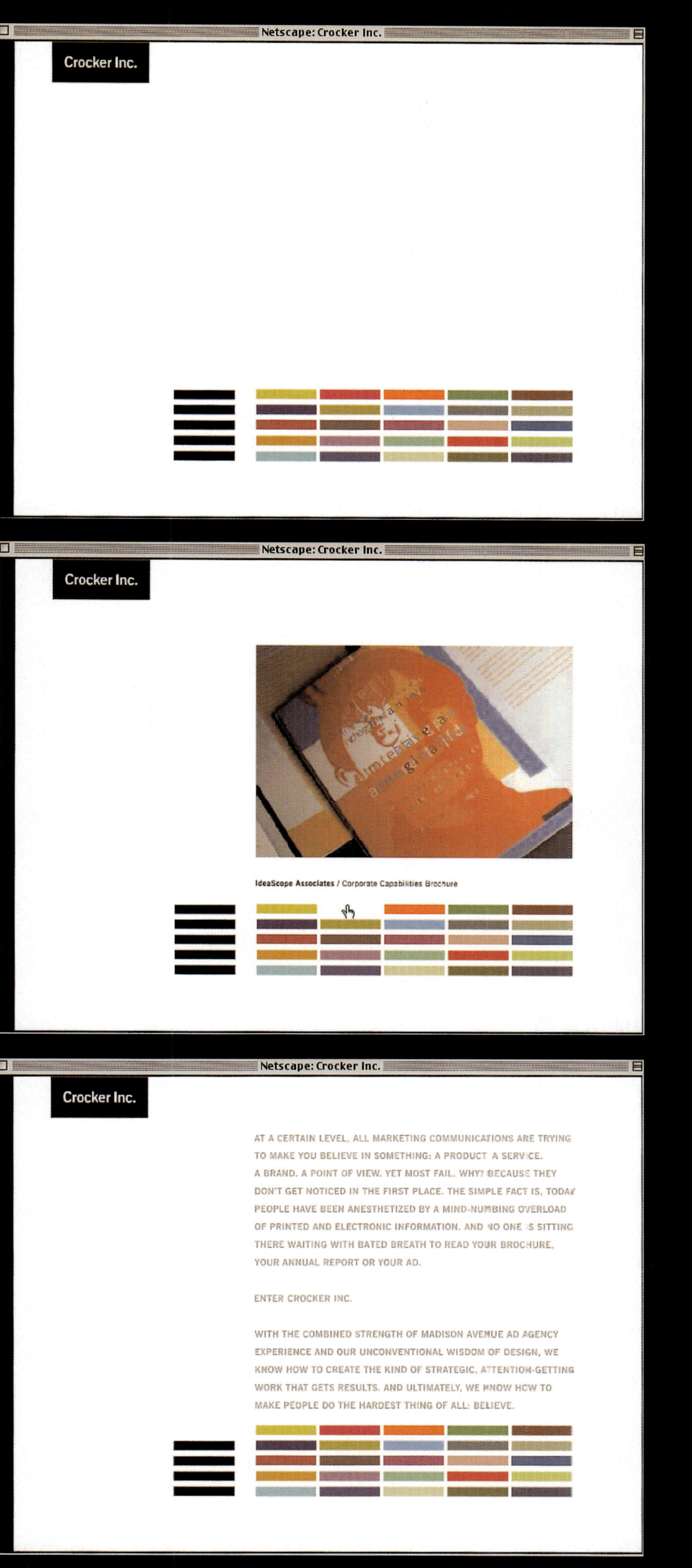

Design Firm **Crocker Inc.** Creative Director **Bruce Crocker** Art Directors **Bruce Crocker** and **James Evelock** Designer and Illustrator **James Evelock** Photographer **Bill Gallery** Copywriter **Jonathan Plazonja** Client **Crocker Inc.**

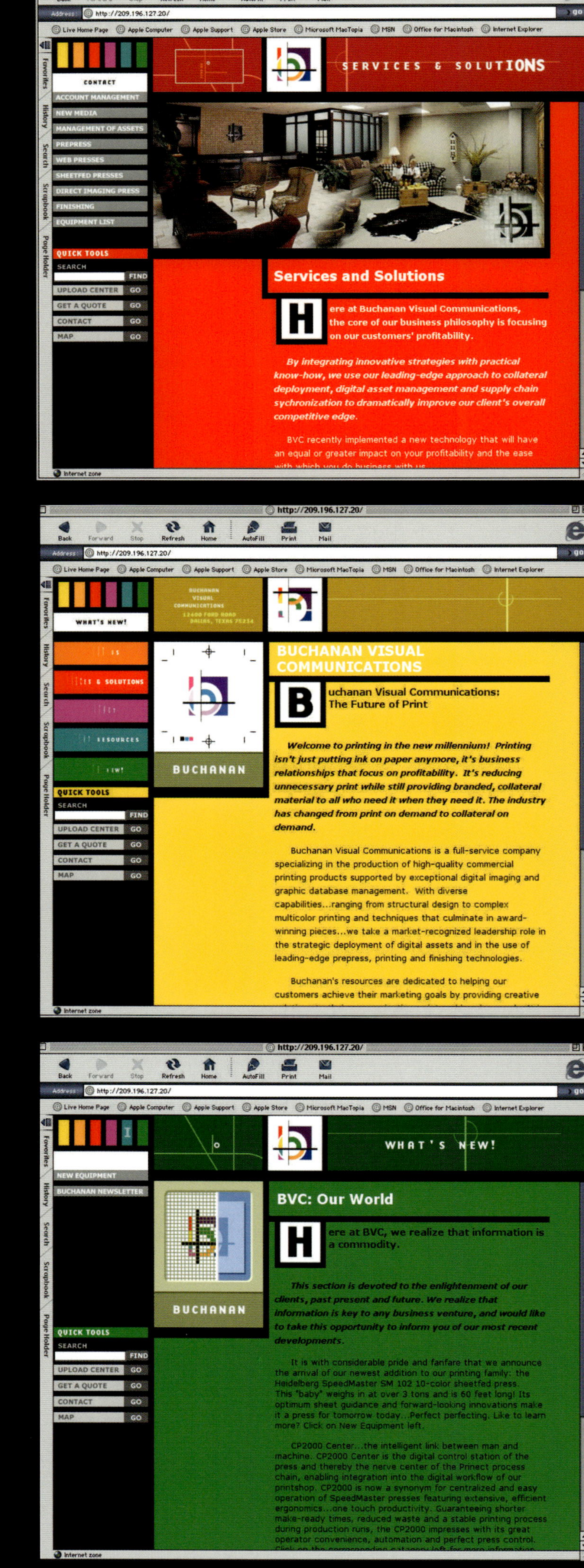

Design Firm **Griffith Phillips** Designer **Brian Niemann** Client **Buchanan Visual Communications**

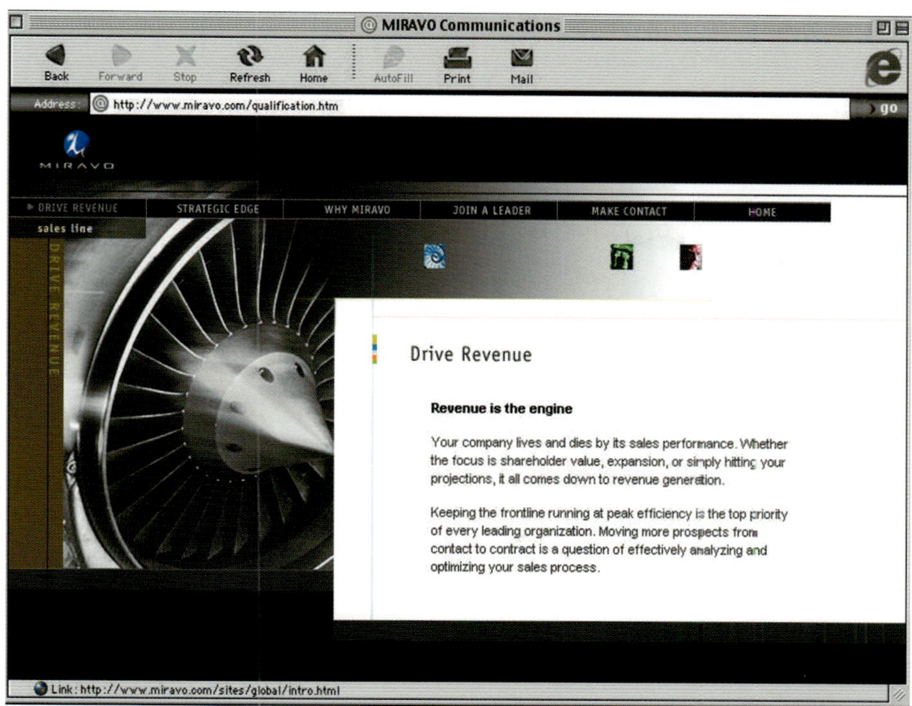

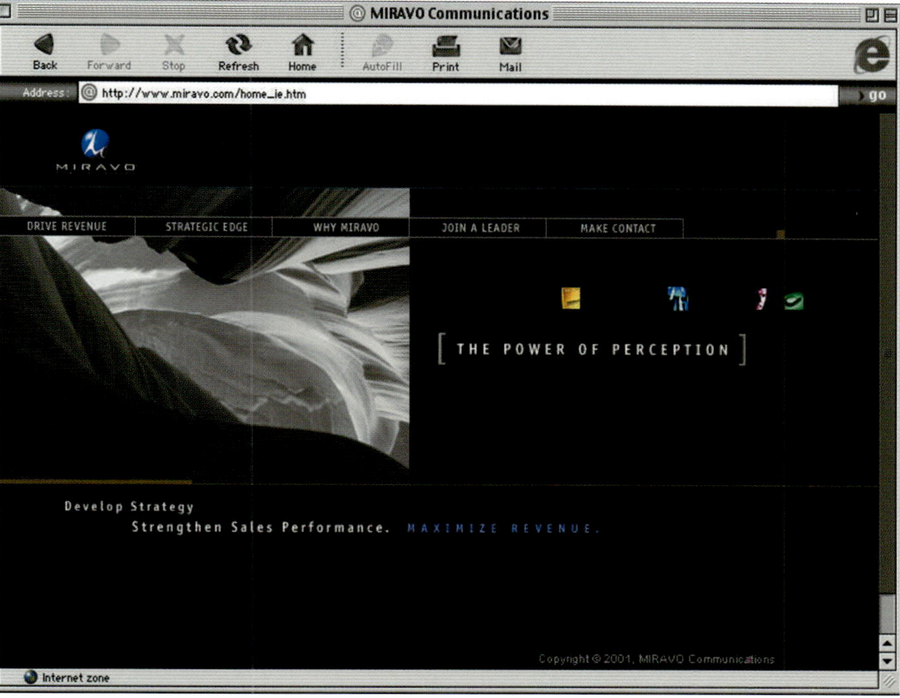

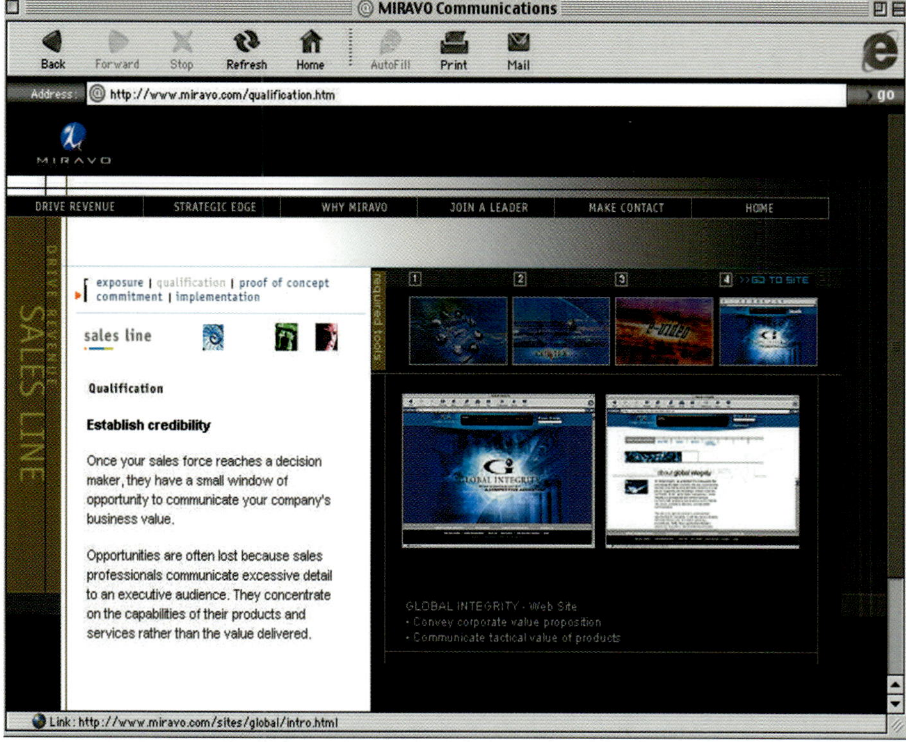

Design Firm **Miravo Communications** Designer **Steve Yasin** Copywriters **Daniel Williford, Rebecca Cressler** and **Ian Bramson** Client **Miravo Communications**

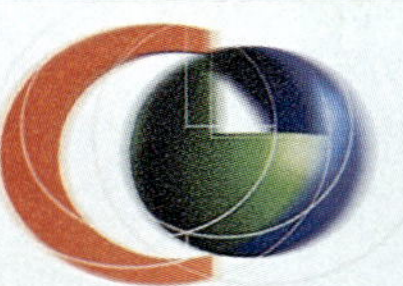

OLC

Oriental Land Co.,Ltd.

1-1Maihama Urayasu-shi Chiba-ken 279-8511 Japan
Tel.047-381-3793 Fax.047-381-3550

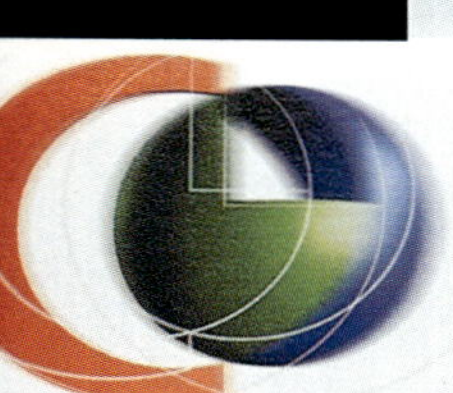

OLC

Oriental Land Co.,Ltd.

1-1Maihama Urayasu-shi Chiba-ken 279-8511 Japan
Tel.047-381-3793 Fax.047-381-3550

OLC

経営企画本部 経営企画室
知画グループ マネージャー

松野 明夫

株式会社オリエンタルランド
279-8511 千葉県浦安市舞浜1-1
Tel 047-305-2063 Fax 047-381-3550

Design Firm **Graphics and Designing Inc.** Art Director, Designer and Illustrator **Toshihiro Onimaru** Client **ODS**

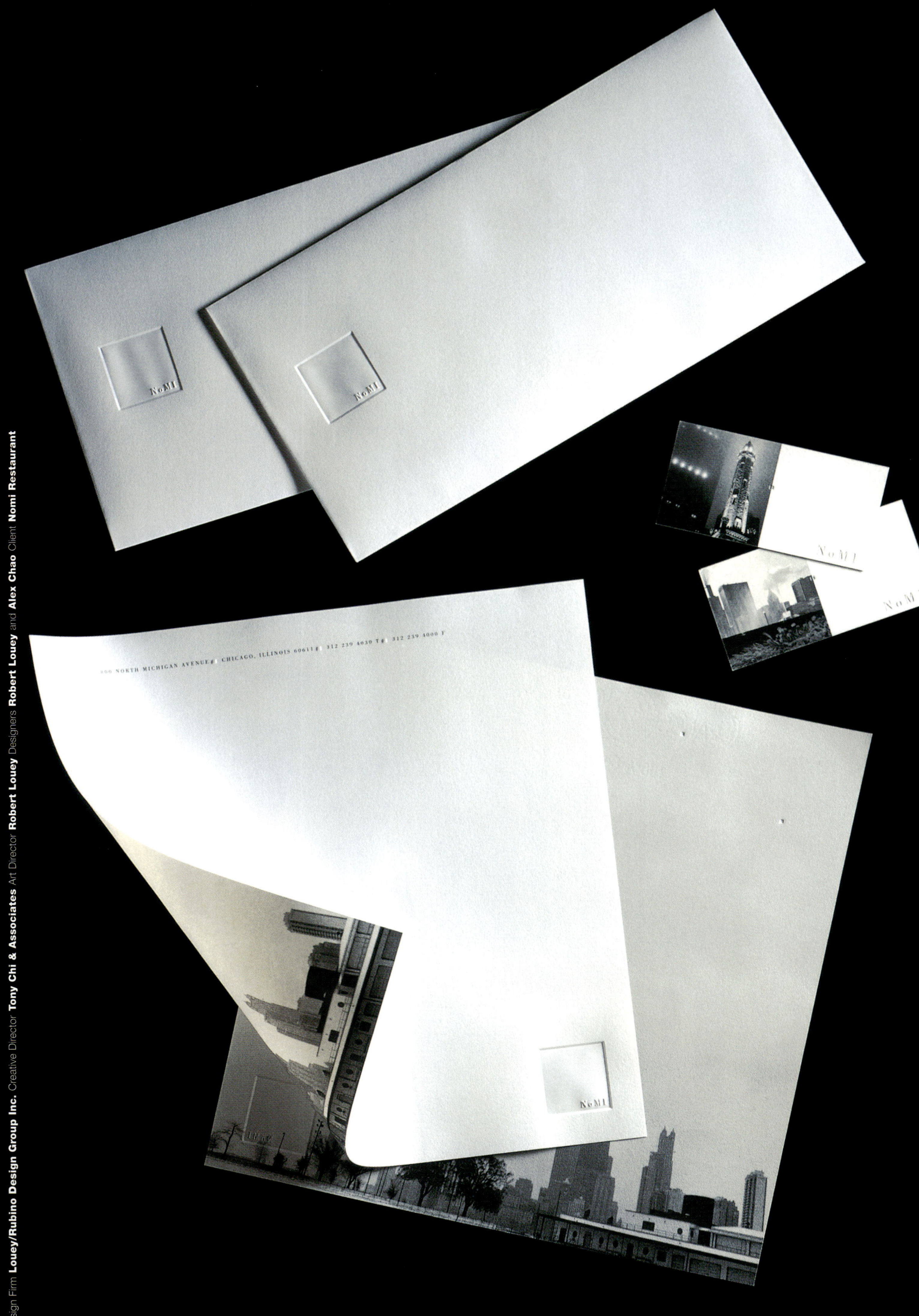

Design Firm **Louey/Rubino Design Group Inc.** Creative Director **Tony Chi & Associates** Art Director **Robert Louey** Designers **Robert Louey** and **Alex Chao** Client **Nomi Restaurant**

Design Firm **Lift Communications, Inc.** Creative Director, Art Director and Designer **Amy Johnson** Photographer **Paul Foster** Client **Half Moon Catering**

(this spread) Design Firm **re:public** Creative Directors **Athena Windelev** and **Morten Windelev** Designer **Athena Windelev** Client **Saga Furs**

Basil Kardasis
Design Director

Sandbjergvej 26
DK-2950 Vedbæk
Denmark
Tel: +45 4565 0088
Fax: +45 4565 0089
Mobile: +45 4040 6614
sidc@sagafurs.com
www.sagafurs.com

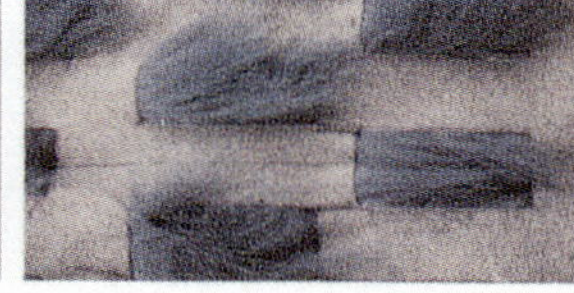

Basil Kardasis
Design Director

Sandbjergvej 26
DK-2950 Vedbæk
Denmark
Tel: +45 4565 0088
Fax: +45 4565 0089
Mobile: +45 4040 6614
sidc@sagafurs.com
www.sagafurs.com

Basil Kardasis
Design Director

Sandbjergvej 26
DK-2950 Vedbæk
Denmark
Tel: +45 4565 0088
Fax: +45 4565 0089
Mobile: +45 4040 6614
sidc@sagafurs.com
www.sagafurs.com

Basil Kardasis
Design Director

Sandbjergvej 26
DK-2950 Vedbæk
Denmark
Tel: +45 4565 0088
Fax: +45 4565 0089
Mobile: +45 4040 6614
sidc@sagafurs.com
www.sagafurs.com

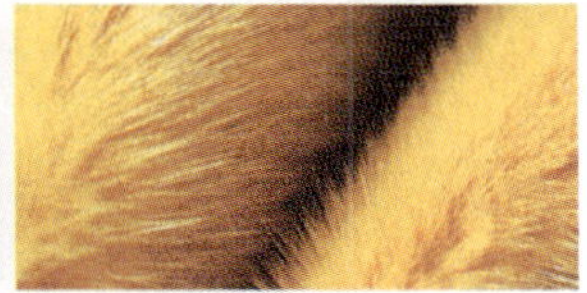

Basil Kardasis
Design Director

Sandbjergvej 26
DK-2950 Vedbæk
Denmark
Tel: +45 4565 0088
Fax: +45 4565 0089
Mobile: +45 4040 6614
sidc@sagafurs.com
www.sagafurs.com

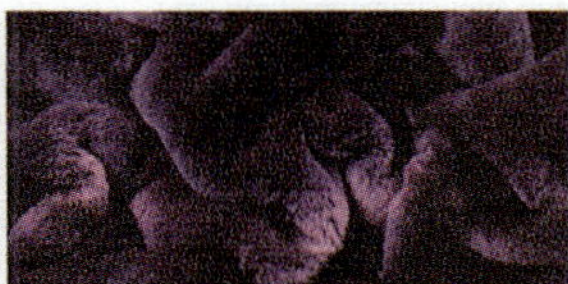

Basil Kardasis
Design Director

Sandbjergvej 26
DK-2950 Vedbæk
Denmark
Tel: +45 4565 0088
Fax: +45 4565 0089
Mobile: +45 4040 6614
sidc@sagafurs.com
www.sagafurs.com

Basil Kardasis
Design Director

Sandbjergvej 26
DK-2950 Vedbæk
Denmark
Tel: +45 4565 0088
Fax: +45 4565 0089
Mobile: +45 4040 6614
sidc@sagafurs.com
www.sagafurs.com

Basil Kardasis
Design Director

Sandbjergvej 26
DK-2950 Vedbæk
Denmark
Tel: +45 4565 0088
Fax: +45 4565 0089
Mobile: +45 4040 6614
sidc@sagafurs.com
www.sagafurs.com

FARMHOUSE
WEB COMPANY

FARMHOUSE
WEB COMPANY

EST.
07071998
1212 BROADWAY NO 822
OAKLAND CA 94612

TYPE
DATE

WWW.FARMHOUSEWEB.COM
EST.
07071998
SEAN MOODY
sean@farmhouseweb.com

EMPLY NO 32187
FARMHOUSE
WEB COMPANY
Serial № 000976
Louise Bartlett
PERSONAL INFO
08.23.00
ST DATE
NO PRESERVATIVES

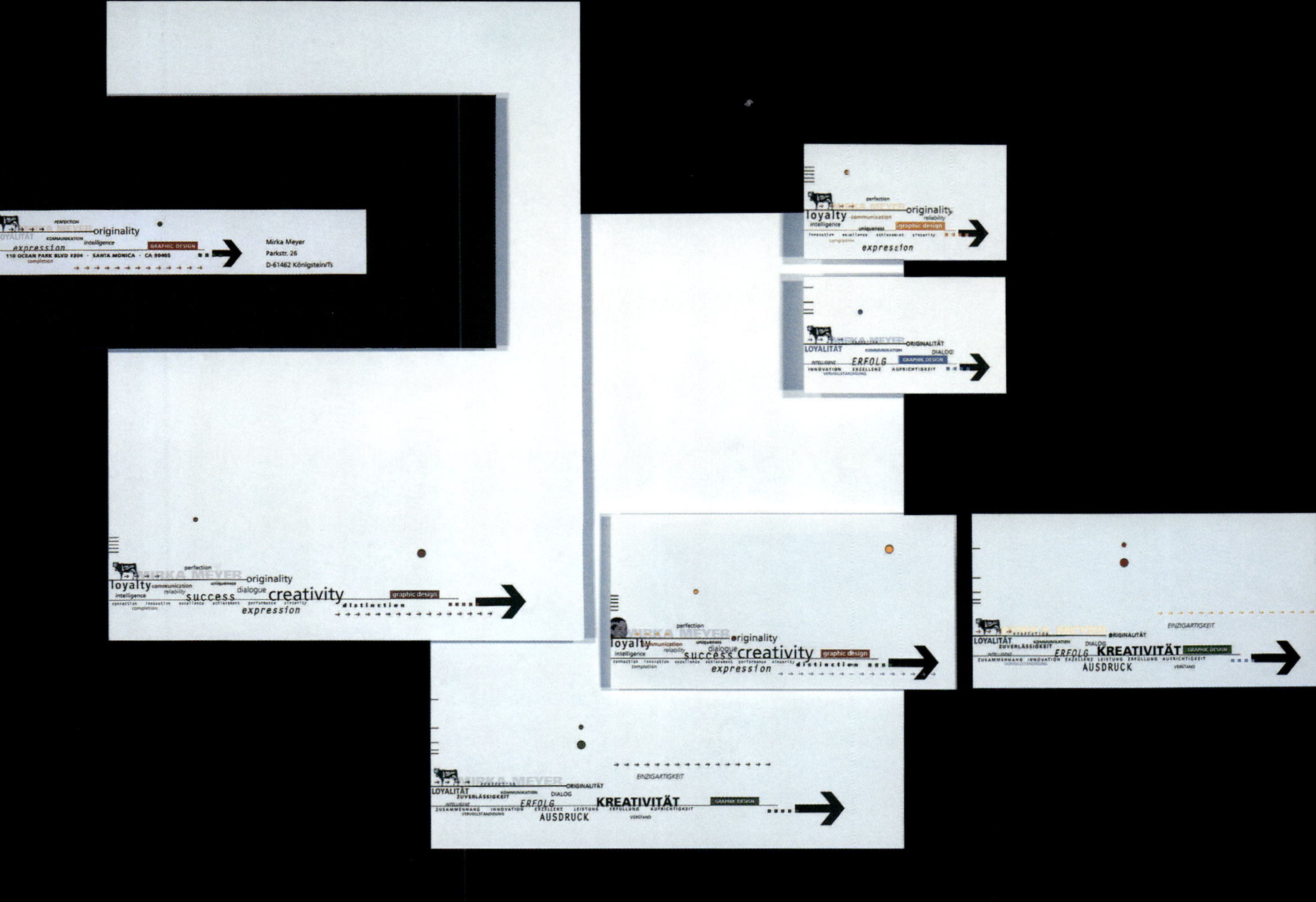

(opposite) Design Firm **Templin Brink Design** Creative Directors **Joel Templin** and **Gaby Brink** Designer **Brian Gunderson** Client **Farmhouse Web Company** (this page) Design Firm **M:C Design Phx:Ffm** Creative Director, Art Director, and Copywriter **Mirka Meyer** Client **Mirka Meyer** (this page) Design Firm **RBMM** Creative Director, Art Director, Designer and Illustrator **Tom Nynas** Client **Public Executions** (opposite, from top) (**1**) Design Firm **Graphics and Designing Inc.** Art Director, Designer and Illustrator **Toshihro Onimaru** Client **ODS** (**2**) Design Firm **Taku Satoh Design Office Inc.** Creative Director **Hiroshi Yonemura** Art Director **Taku Satoh** Designers **Taku Satoh** and **Ichiji Ohishi** Client **Asahi Satellite Broadcasting Limited** (**3**) Design Firm **Turner Duckworth** Creative Directors **David Turner** and **Bruce Duckworth** Designers **David Turner** and **Jonathan Warner** Photographers **Michael Lamotte** and **Martin Schoeller** Client **Palm Inc.** (**4**) Design Firm **Mires Design, Inc.** Creative and Art Director **José Serrano** Designer **Miguel Pérez** Illustrator **Fermin Mateo-Cruz** Client **Borrelli** (**5**) Design Firm **Sandstrom Design** Creative Director **Steve Sandstrom** Art Director and Designer **Dan Richards** Client **800.com**

palm
™

PARK BLVD
MICHAEL BORRELLI
ARTS AND CRAFTS
ARTWORKS

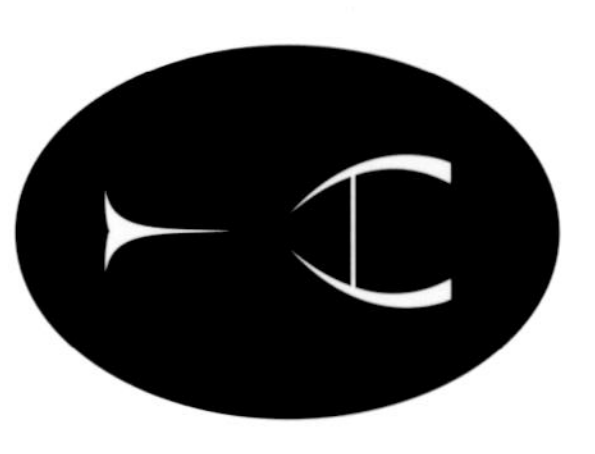

(from top) (**1**) Design Firm **RBMM** Creative Director, Art Director, Designer and Illustrator **Tom Nynas** Client **Domaine Haleaux** (**2**) Design Firm **Direct Design Studio** Creative Directors **Dmitry Pioryshkov** and **Leonid Feigin** Client **Insurance Department of the Oil Company "Yucos"** (**3**) Design Firm **Ambrosini Design** Creative and Art Director **Ken Ambrosini** Designers **Ken Ambrosini** and **Dardinelle Troen** Client **GSL Properties** (**4**) Designer **Mark Braught** Client **Hubbard Publicity** (**5**) Design Firm **RBMM** Creative Director **Dick Mitchell** Art Director, Designer and Illustrator **Tom Nynas** Client **Rams (High School Basketball Team)**

Design Firm **Brian J. Ganton & Associates** Creative Director **Brian Ganton Jr.** Art Director and Designer **Christopher Ganton** Illustrator **Juan Lee** Client **United States Tobacco International**

(this page) Designers **Libby Delana** and **Mark Yurkew** Photographer **Bruce Peterson** (opposite, from top) (**1**) Design Firms **Chaney, Nieman, Munson & Son** and **Catapult Strategic Design** Art Director **Milo Munson** Designer and Illustrator **Randy Heil** Client **Catapult** (**2**) Design Firm **Sibley Peteet Design** Art Director **Matt Heck** Designer and Illustrator **David Guillory** Client **Mother Hen Software** (**3**) Design Firm **Graphics and Designing Inc.** Art Director and Designer **Toshihro Onimaru** Client **George's Furniture Co., Ltd.** (**4**) Design Firm **Mires Design, Inc.** Creative and Art Director **José Serrano** Designer **Miguel Perez** Client **Yellow Pages** (**5**) Design Firm **yellobee Studio** Art Director and Illustrator **Alison Scheel** Client **Chase Food Company**

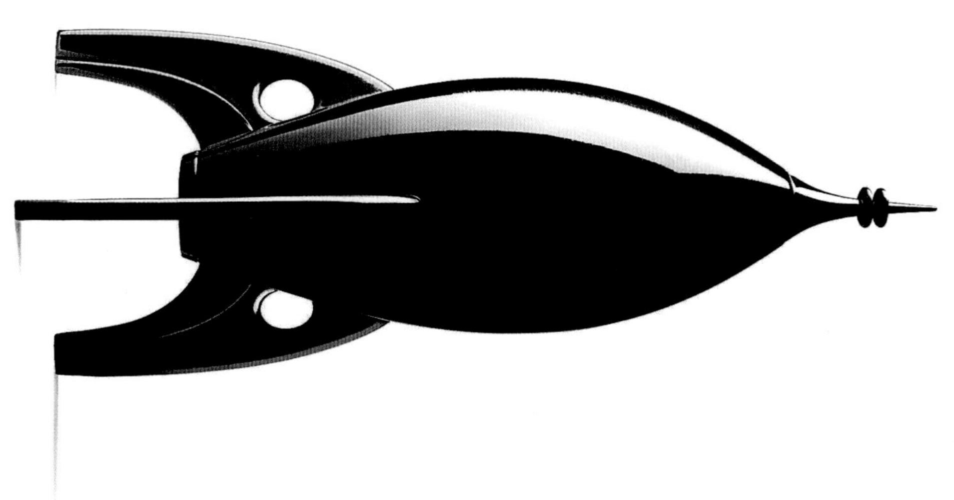

CATAPULT

GEORGE'S

TM

CHASE FOOD
FRESH RECIPES
HEALTHY FOOD
COMPANY

(from top) (**1**) Design Firm **Thinking Caps** Creative and Art Directors **Julie Henson** and **Ann Morton** Designer **Rolando Gumler** Client **DWL** (**2**) Design Firm **Brainforest** Creative Director and Designer **Nils Bunde** Client **Gus Berthold Electric Company** (**3**) Design Firm **Hvita Husid** Creative Director, Art Director and Designer **Kristin Thora Gudbjartsdottir** Client **The Association of Icelandic Insurance Companies** (**4**) Design Firm **RBMM** Creative Director, Art Director, Designer and Illustrator **Tom Nynas** Client **Lionsgate Communications** (**5**) Design Firm **RBMM** Designer **Dan Birlew** Client **Triclops**

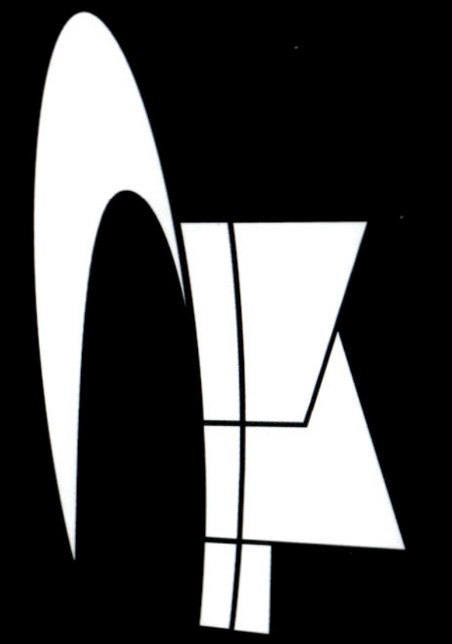

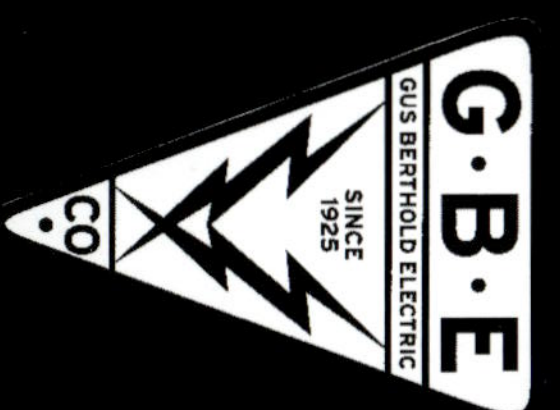

Design Firm **BGX Limited** Creative Director **Simon Siu** Art Director **Dominic Chan** Client **Nokia (Hong Kong)**

(this page) Design Firm **Sibley Peteet Design** Creative Director **Tim McClure** Art Director and Designer **Mark Brinkman** Illustrators **Mark Brinkman** and **Rex Peteet** Client **Barton Creek Country Club** (opposite, from top) (**1**) Design Firm **Greenwich Design Associates** Designer **Simon Wright** Illustrator **Liz Herring** Client **Shell Aviation** (**2**) Design Firm **Hornall Anderson Design Works, Inc.** Art Director **Jack Anderson** Designers **Jack Anderson, Lisa Cerveny, Don Stayner** and **Mary Chin Hutchison** Client **Twelve Horses** (**3**) Design Firm **GSD&M** Creative Director **Marty Erhart** Art Director **Patrick Nolan** Designers **Patrick Nolan** and **Kevin Peake** Illustrator **Kevin Peake** Copywriter **Clay Hudson** Client **Theme Park** (**4**) Design Firm **Creative Soup, Inc.** Creative Director, Designer and Illustrator **Mark Wilcox** Client **Cambridge Carpet** (**5**) Design Firm **Kellum McClain, Inc.** Creative Director **John Athorn** Designer **Ron Kellum** Client **Athorn Clark & Partners**

TWELVE HORSES

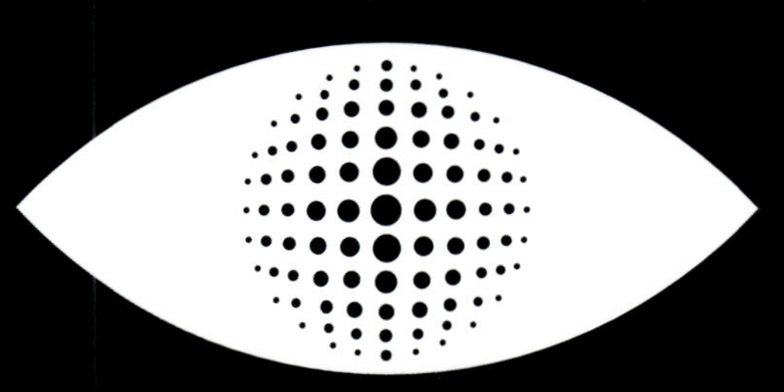

THE PORTRAIT
RESTAURANT
Menu

THE PORTRAIT
RESTAURANT

THE PORTRAIT
RESTAURANT

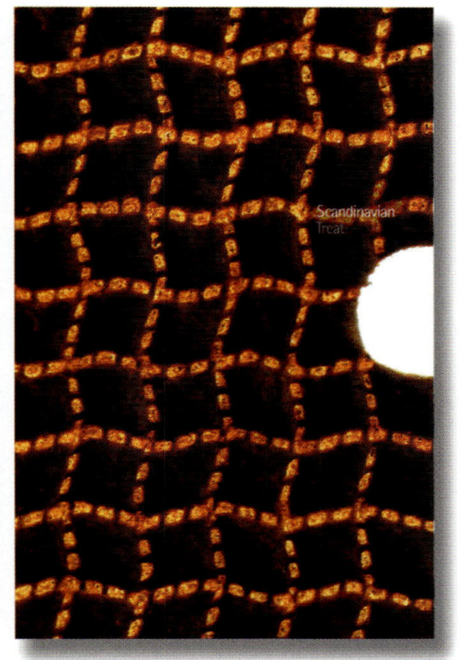

Design Firm **Intellecta Corporate** Art Director and Designer **Anders Schmidt** Photographer **Roland Persson** Client **SAS (Scandinavian Airlines)**

Design Firm **Kellerhouse, Inc.** Creative and Art Directors **Neil Kellerhouse** and **Steve Gerdes** Designer **Neil Kellerhouse** Photographers **Neil Kellerhouse** and **Jeff Jones** Illustrator **Rohan** Copywriter **Liza Gerberding** Client **Reprise Records. A Time Warner Company**

Design Firm **be_poles** Creative Director **Patrice Lourme** Art Director **Antoine Ricardou** Designer **Clementine De Mesties** Illustrator **Don Coley** Client **Andante**

Design Firm **Sony Music** Art Director **Mary Maurer** Designers **Mary Maurer, Doug Erb** and **Brandy Flower** Photographers **Rocky Schenk, Marty Temme, Brandy Flower, Paul Hernandez, Catherine Wessel, Dennis Keely, Karen Manson, Steffan Chirazi** and **Peter Fletcher**

Director **Stefan Sagmeister** Designer and Illustrator **Motoko Hada** Photographer **Danny Clinch** Client **Radioactive Records**

106 nine
THE CITY
106 nine
THE CITY

Design Firm **Sullivan Perkins** Designer and Illustrator **Kelly Allen** Copywriters **Michael Langley** and **Mark Perkins** Client **The Dallas Public Library**

Design Firm **Taku Satoh Design Office Inc.** Art Director **Taku Satoh** Designers **Taku Sahoh** and **Shino Misawa** Client **P.G.C.D. Japan Inc.**

Design Firm **Taku Satoh Design Office Inc.** Creative Directors **Minoru Shiokawa** and **Taku Satoh** Art Director **Taku Satoh** Designer **Kazutoshi Amano** Client **FT Shiseido Co., Ltd.**

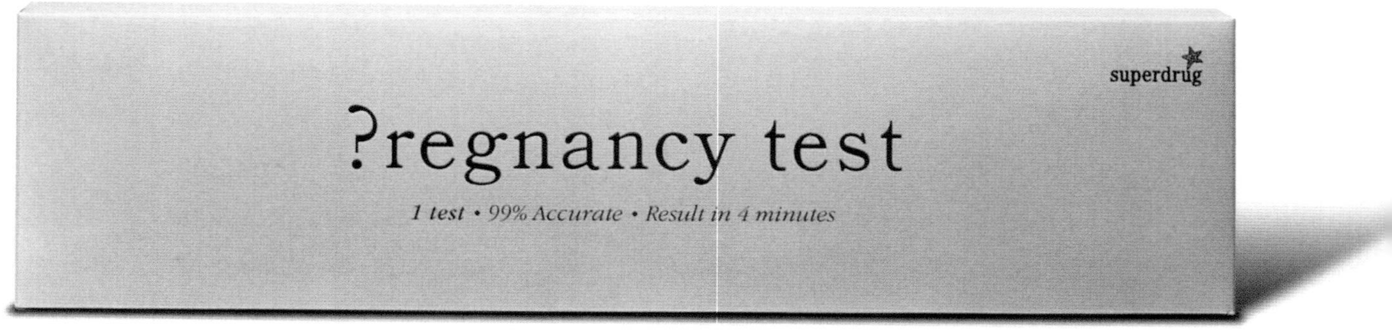

superdrug

?regnancy test

1 test • 99% Accurate • Result in 4 minutes

Design Firm **Williams Murray Hamm** Creative Director **Garrick Hamm** Designer **Clare Pompard** Client **Superdrug**

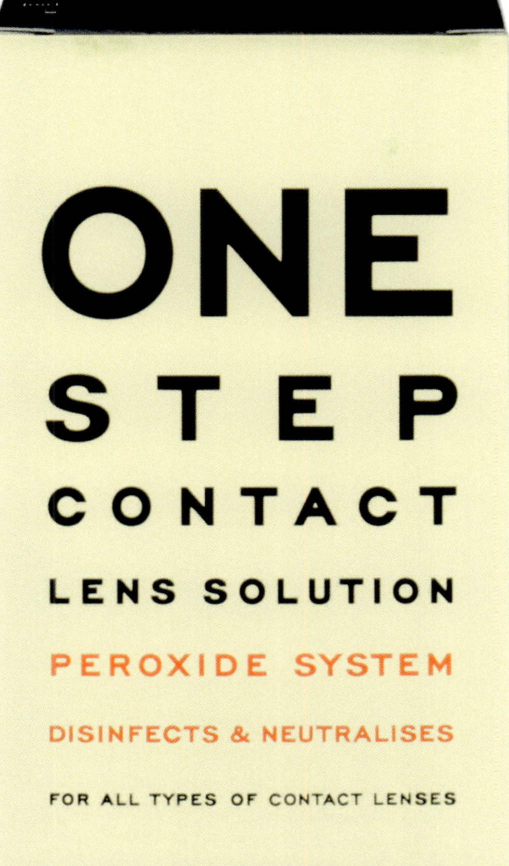

Design Firm **Williams Murray Hamm** Creative Director **Garrick Hamm** Designer **Fiona Curran** Copywriter **Richard Murray** Client **Superdrug**

Design Firm **Butler, Shine & Stern** Creative Director **John Butler** Designer **Suzanne Shade** Copywriter **Nicole Michels** Client **Nuance**

Design Firm **Sandstrom Design** Creative Director **Steve Sandstrom** Art Director and Designer **Jon Olsen** Illustrator **Jeff Foster** Copywriter **Leslee Dillon** Client **Hollywood Entertainment**

Design Firm **P.P.I.C.** Creative Director, Art Director and Copywriter **Tetsuji Kawamura** Designer and Illustrator **Suzuko Hirata** Photographer **Katsutoshi Motomatsu** Client **Nakashima Chochin Co. Ltd.**

Design Firm **Packaging Create Inc.** Art Director and Designer **Akio Okumura** Client **Inter Medium Institute Graduate School** (this spread) Design Firm **Sandstrom Design** Creative Director **Steve Sandstrom** Art Director and Designer **Jon Olsen** Illustrator **Larry Jost** Copywriter **Leslee Dillon** Client **Castor & Pollux Pet Products**

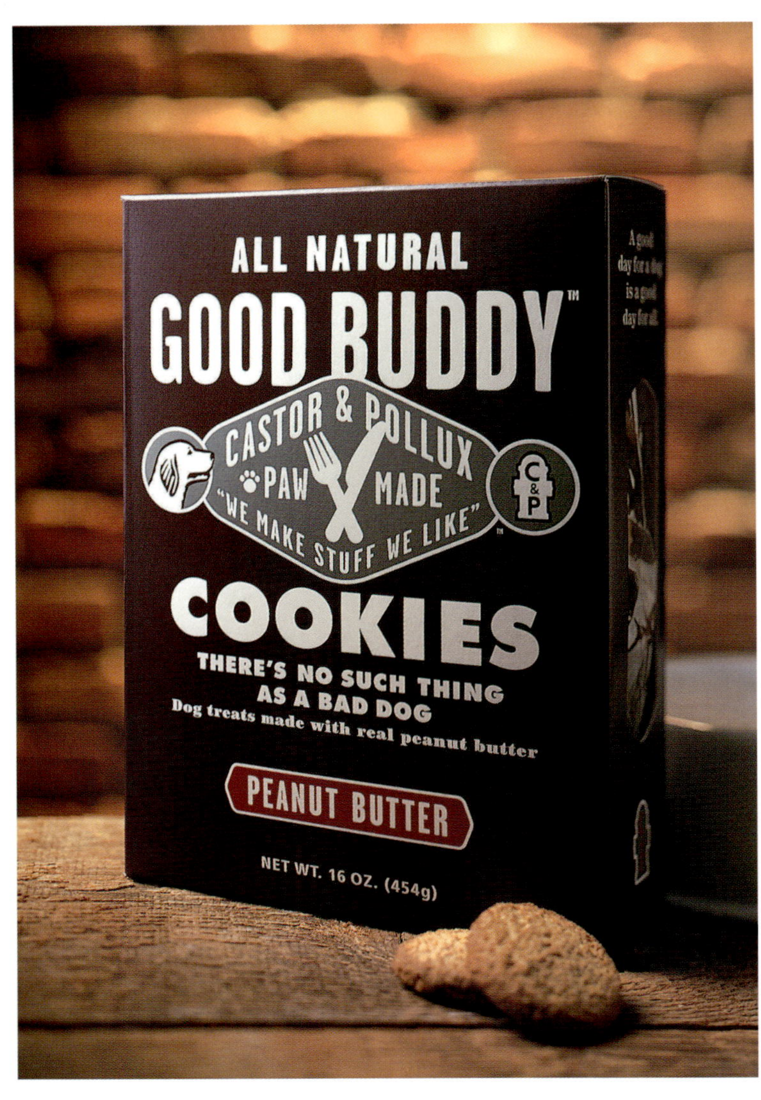

PRESSED
WET NOSE™
PAW MADE
C&P
7-PAK
280-315 gm
KNOTTED
WET NOSE™
CASTOR & POLLUX
PAW MADE
C&P
RAWHIDE
TREAT YOUR DOG RIGHT
7-PAK
CONVENIENT SEVEN DAY MINI PAK
Be a small dog's best friend
every day of the week.
SEVEN 2.5" KNOTTED
SUN-DRIED RAWHIDE BONES

Design Firm **Blattner Brunner** Creative Director **Rodney Underwood** Art Director and Designer **David Vissat** Illustrator **Livia Evans** Client **Best Feeds**

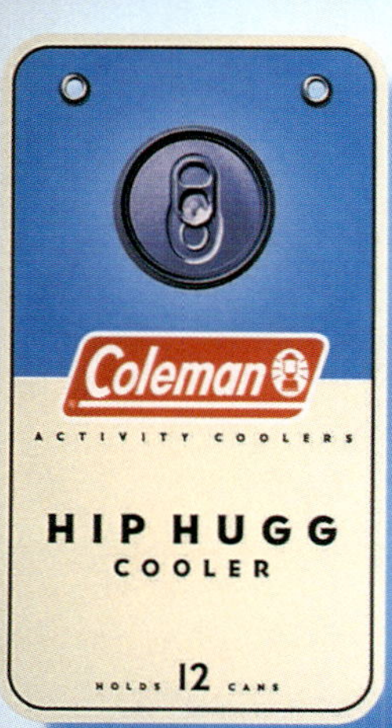

Design Firm **Landor Associates** Creative Director **Nicolas Aparicio** Art Director **Christopher Lehmann** Designers **Anastasia Laksmi** and **Philip Foster** Photographer **Michael Friel** Client **The Coleman Company**

Design Firm **Pentagram Design** Art Director **Kit Hinrichs** Designers **Erik Schmitt** and **Kit Hinrichs** Client **NapaStyle**

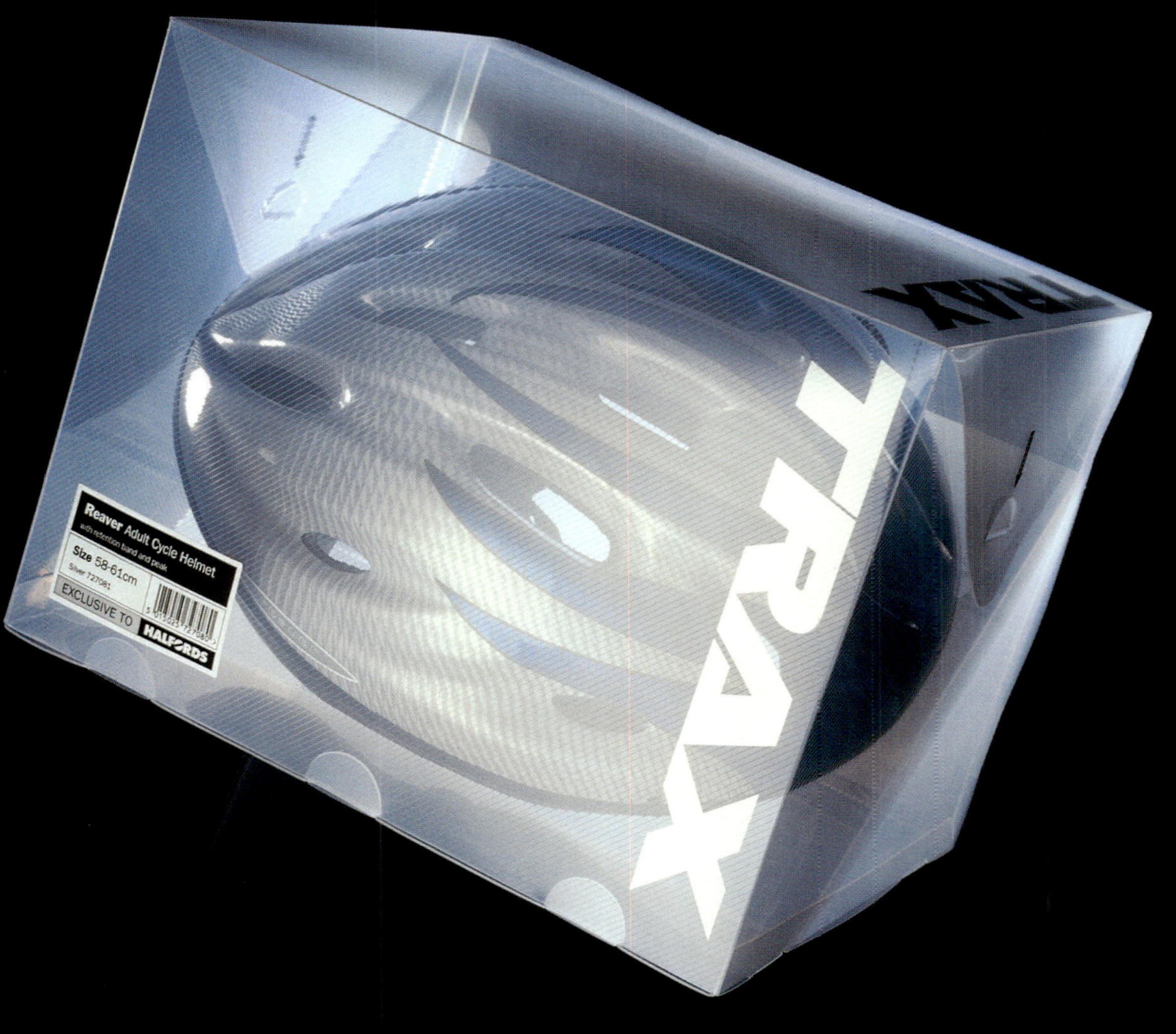

Design Firm **Lippa Pearce Design Ltd.** Creative Directors **Harry Pearce** and **Domenic Lippa** Art Director **Harry Pearce** Designers **Harry Pearce** and **Jeremy Roots** Client **Halfords Limited**

Design Firm **Atelier Haase & Knels** Creative Director **Harald Schweers** Art Director and Designer **Katja Hirschfelder** Client **Stanwell Vertriebs GmbH**

Design Firm **Sandstrom Design** Creative Director, Art Director, Designer and Illustrator **Steve Sandstrom** Copywriter **Steve Sandoz** Client **Tazo**

Ginger & Lemongrass
Bliss
Ginger & Lemongrass
Orange Blossom & Grapefruit
Renewal
PHARMACOPIA
Orange Blossom & Grapefruit
Purifying Body Oil
PHARMACOPIA
Rosemary, Lavender & Juniper
Invigorating Bath Salts
PHARMACOPIA
Rosemary & Mint
PHARMACOPIA
Lemongrass, Ginger & Cinnamon
Radiating Bath Salts
Lavender & Chamomile
Soothing Bath Salts
PHARMACOPIA
Orange Blossom, Tangerine & Grapefruit
Restorative Bath Salts
Rosemary & Mint
Energy
Rosemary & Mint
PHARMACOPIA
Ginger & Lemongrass
Muscle-Soothing Oil
PHARMACOPIA
Lavender & Chamomile
Relaxing Body Oil
Lavender & Tea Tree
Serenity
Lavender & Tea Tree

(top) Design Firm **Kilmer & Kilmer** Creative Director **Richard Kilmer** Designer **Randall Marshall** Client **Kilmer & Kilmer** (bottom) Design Firm **Insight Design Communications** Creative Director, Art Director and Designer **Sherrie Holdeman** and **Tracy Holdeman** Client **With A Twist** (top left) Design Firm **Britton Design** Creative Director, Art Director and Designer **Patti Britton** Client **Hermitage Road** (top right) Design Firm **Stromme Throndsen Design** Creative Director **Morten Throndsen** Designers **Morten Throndsen** and **Ela Grodal** Client **Ringnes** (bottom left) Design Firm **Williams Murray Hamm** Creative Director **Garrick Hamm** Designer and Illustrator **Fiona Curran** Client **Heals Department Store** (bottom right) Design Firm **Klim Design, Inc.** Creative and Art Director **Matt Klim** Designers **Matt Klim** and **Marcus Klim** Photographer **Greg Klim** Client **Bols Royal Distilleries**

Design Firm **Selbert Perkins Design** Creative Director **Robin Perkins** Art Director **Georgia Robrecht** Client **Eurobubblies**

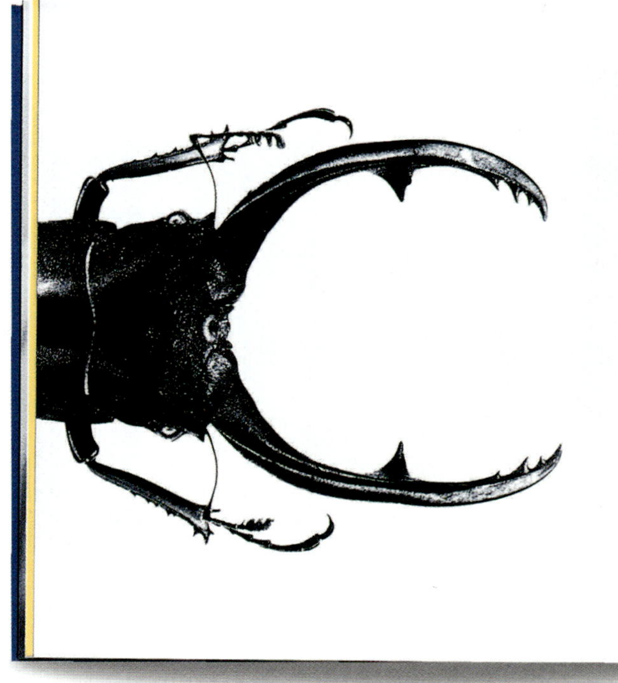

(this spread) Design Firm **Navy Blue Design** Creative Director **Jon Evans** Designers **Judith Reid** and **Iain Valentine** Copywriters **Jon Evans** and **P. Evans** Clients **Strathmore Papers** and **GF Smith**

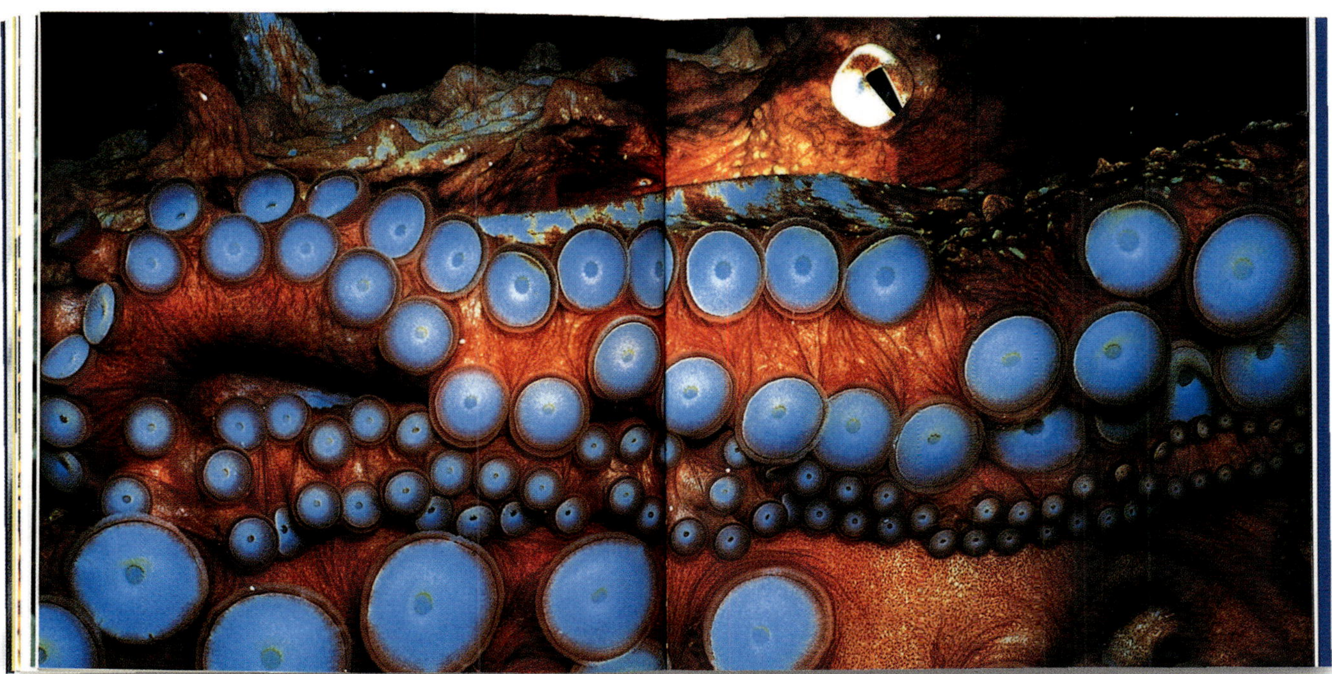

Design Firm **Nippon Design Center, Inc.** Art Director **Kazumasa Nagai** Client **Takeo Co., Ltd.**

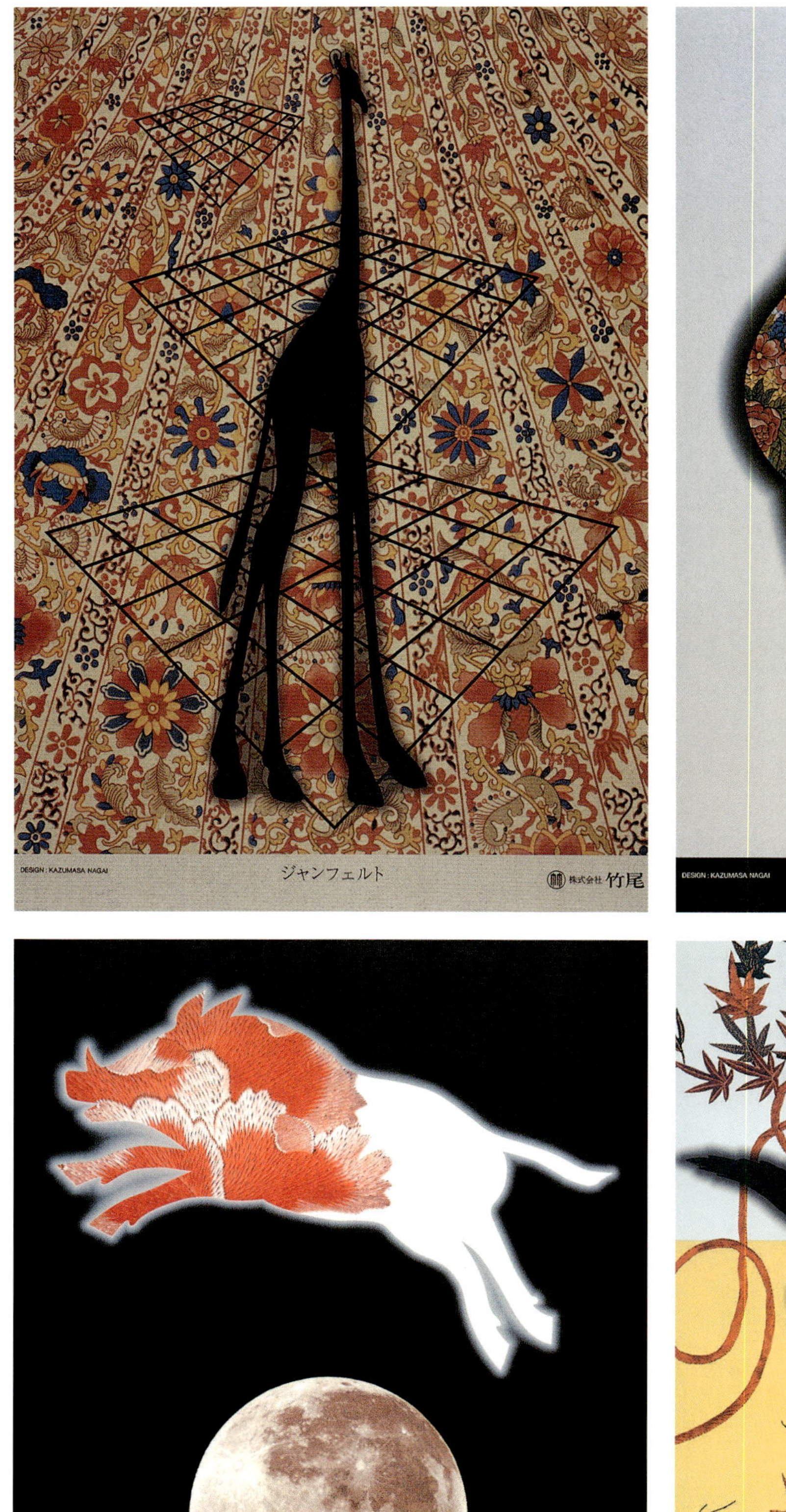

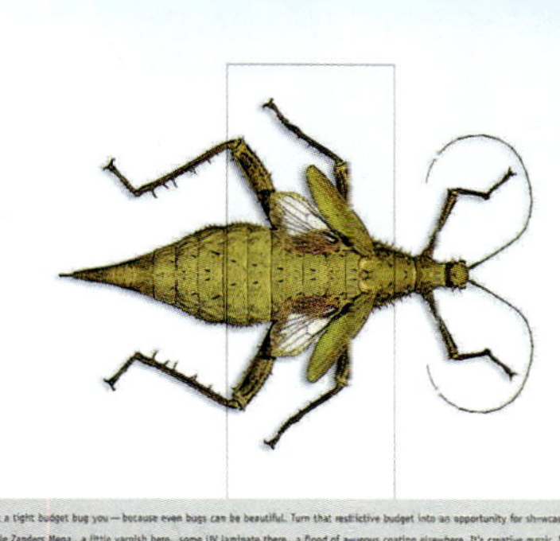

This Spread: Dry-trapped gloss and dull varnish over 4/c process images, dull UV laminate within borders and over solid match colors, in-line gloss varnish over screened match colors.

Don't let a tight budget bug you—because even bugs can be beautiful. Turn that restrictive budget into an opportunity for showcasing your creativity. Affordable Zanders Mega...a little varnish here...some UV laminate there...a flood of aqueous coating elsewhere. It's creative magic. It's *Megomorphosis*.

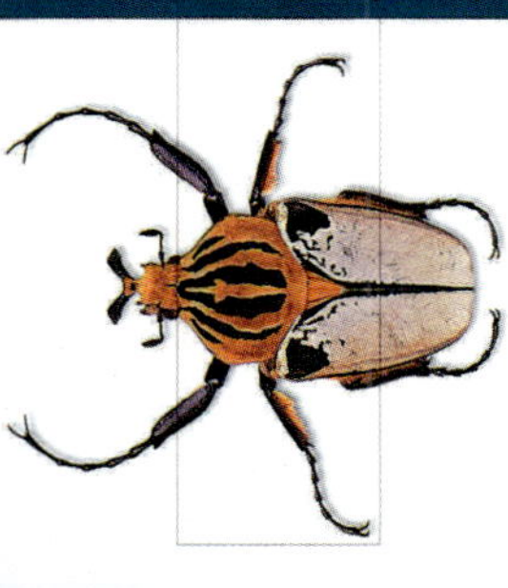

Zanders Mega Gloss 115 lb Text

Varnishes. UV laminates. Aqueous coatings. Use them in-line over wet ink for subtle effects. Use them off-line over dry ink for a more pronounced effect. Tint them with color and apply them directly to the paper for a subtle suggestion of an image that shimmers in the light. However you use these on-press gloss and dull finishing techniques, they'll add creativity and interest to your printed piece.

Zanders Mega Gloss 115 lb Text

Left Page: Dry-trapped gloss and dull varnish over match text with gloss UV laminate over 4/c process and "Mega."
This Page: In-line tinted dull varnish halftones with dry-trapped gloss varnish over 4/c process images.

Zanders Mega Dull 115 lb Text

This Page: Dry-trapped gloss varnish over 4/c process images, in-line tinted dull varnish overprinting light contrast quadratone, dry-trapped gloss and dull varnish within border.

Right Page: Dry-trapped silver tinted varnish and gloss UV laminate over 4/c process image with dry-trapped gloss, dull and silver tinted varnish over process black.

Is this the way you sometimes picture your client? There's really no need for that. Just use some of the techniques you see here and change that image. It's classic *Megomorphosis*...and it happens only on Zanders Mega.

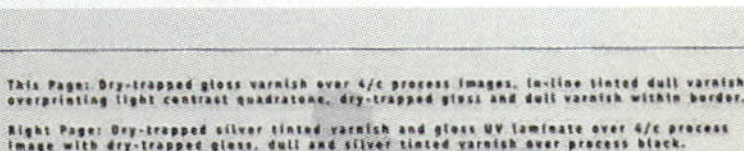

Zanders Mega Gloss 115 lb Text

Zanders Mega Dull 115 lb Text

(this spread) Design Firm **João Machado Design Ltd.** Creative Director, Art Director, Designer and Illustrator **João Machado** Client **Gabinete Deapoio Empressarial Do Vale Do**

2000

PAPÉIS CARREIRA

2000

PAPÉIS CARREIRA

2000

PAPÉIS CARREIRA

2000

PAPÉIS CARREIRA

3
Lamego
de
2000

Congresso Portugal-Brasil
Ano 2000
Faculdade de Letras Porto
12-14 de Junho de 2000

2001
D
P
PAPÉIS CARREIRA

2001
D
P
PAPÉIS CARREIRA

BLUE

Josef Albers David Austen Glenn Brown Anthony Caro Patrick Caulfield Marc Chagall Tony Cragg Muirne Kate Dineen Felim Egan Sylvie Fleury Lucian Freud Andrew Gifford Barbara Hepworth Damien Hirst Callum Innes Derek Jarman Anish Kapoor Kazuo Katase Keith Khan and Ali Zaidi (moti roti) Yves Klein Maria Lalić Peter Lanyon René Magritte Franz Marc Jason Martin Joan Miró David Nash Mariele Neudecker Pablo Picasso Bridget Riley Julie Roberts Yuko Shiraishi Alice Stepanek and Steven Maslin EstelleThompson Andy Warhol Richard Wentworth James White and Tim Sheward

BLUE: borrowed and new 16th February - May 2000
The opening exhibition of The New Art Gallery Walsall
Tuesday - Saturday 10am-5pm Sunday 12noon-5pm
Closed Monday Open Bank Holidays
The New Art Gallery Walsall, Gallery Square
Walsall, West Midlands WS2 8LG
T 01922 654400 F 01922 654401 www.artatwalsall.org.uk

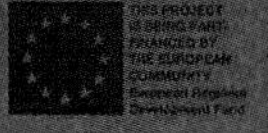

HSBC

Design Firm **Michael Nash Associates** Art Directors and Designers **Anthony Michael, Stephanie Nash** and **Jane Chipchase** Photographer **Derek Hillier** Client **The New Art Gallery**

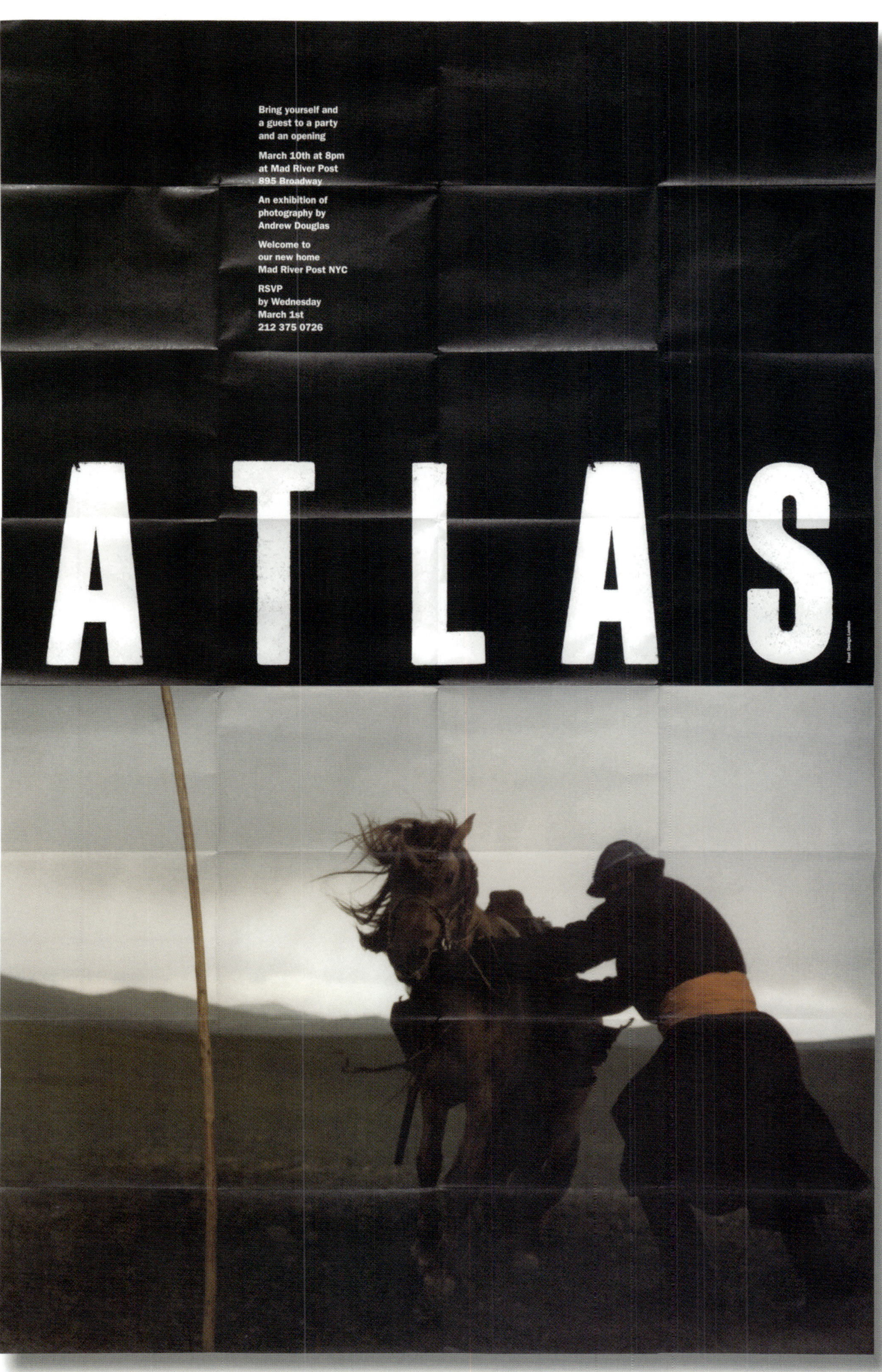

Design Firm **Frost Design** Creative Director, Art Director and Designer **Vince Frost** Photographer **Andrew Douglas** Client **Andrew Douglas**

Satoh Design Office Inc. Art Director and Designer **Taku Satoh** Photographer **Kazumi Kurigami** Client **Tokyo Art Directors Club**

Design Firm **Pentagram Design, Inc.** Art Director **D. J. Stout** Designers **Brett Carter** and **D. J. Stout** Client **D. J. Stout**

(this spread) Design Firm **HEBE Werbung & Design** Creative Director, Art Director and Copywriter **Reiner Hebe** Client **Schuhhaus Werdich GmbH & Co.**

Workhorse Advertising Creative Directors **Tim Abare** and **Chris Beatty** Designers **David Bellamy** and **Chris Beatty** Copywriter **Tim Abare** Client **Workhorse Advertising**

package-land.com

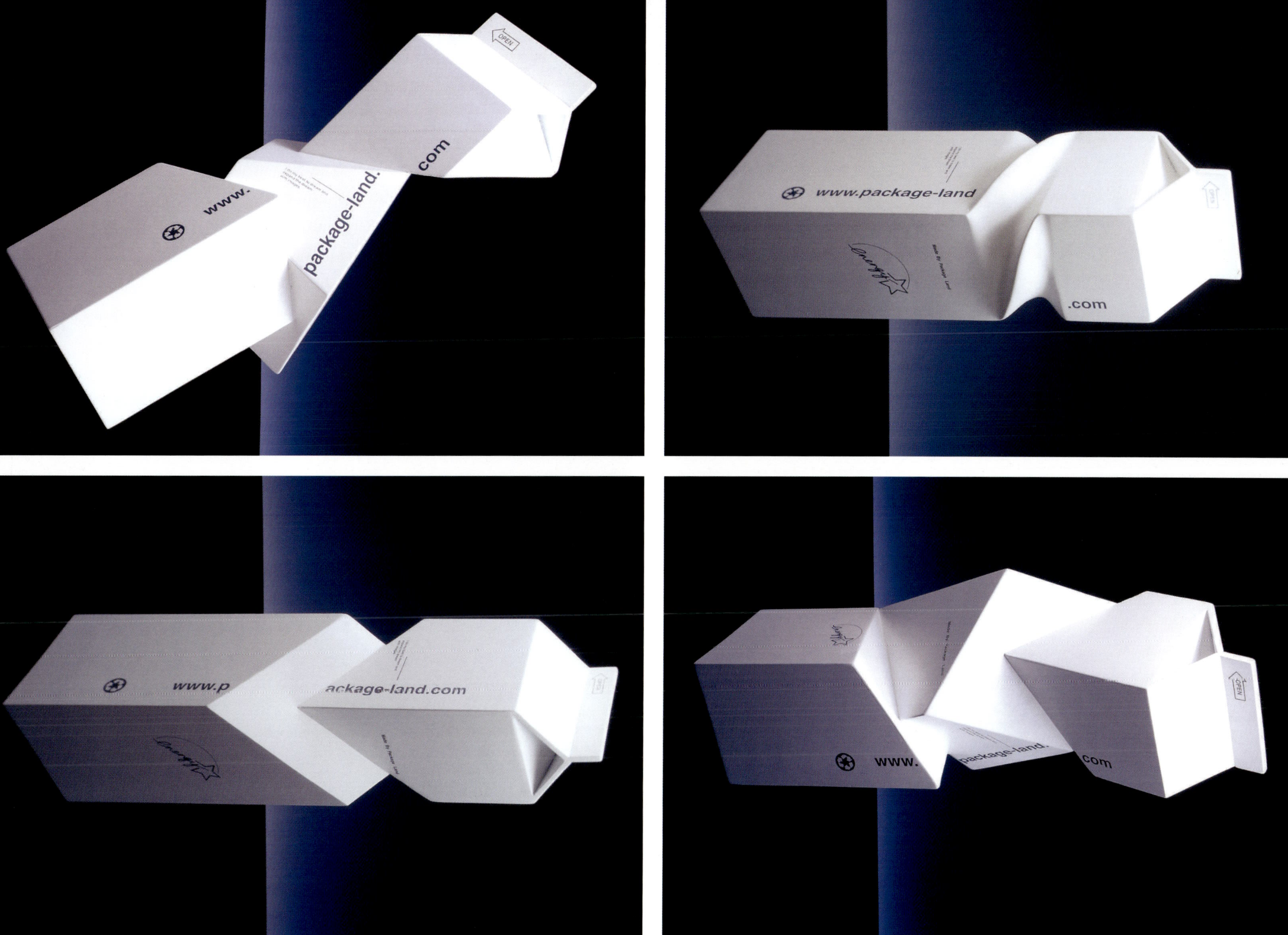

(this spread) Design Firm **Package Land Co., Ltd.** Art Director, Designer and Photographer **Yasuo Tanaka** Client **Package Land Co., Ltd.**

Design Firm **Wallace Church, Inc.** Creative Director **Stan Church** Art Directors **David Minkley** and **Wendy Church** Designer and Copywriter **David Minkley** Photographer **David Lyons** Illustrator **Michael Scaraglino** Client **Wallace Church Inc.**

Design Firm **SS Studio** Art Director, Designer and Photographer **Sayuri Shoji** Client **Issey Miyake, Inc.**

Design Firm **Brann Richmond** Creative Director **John Lindner** Designer **James Sweeney** Copywriter **Linda Snyder** Client **Brann Richmond**

Sooner
or late
all
direct ma
faces
the sam
test.

If it
ends up
here,
it's not
from us.

BRANN

Unfortunately,
it may
not be the
response
you're
looking fo

Talk to us. We're listening.

Any
direct marketing
can give you a strong
response.

Design Firm **Tom Fowler, Inc.** Creative Director **Thomas G. Fowler** Art Director **Karl S. Maruyama** Designer **Brien O'Reilly** Client **Eventra**

Knohoholl

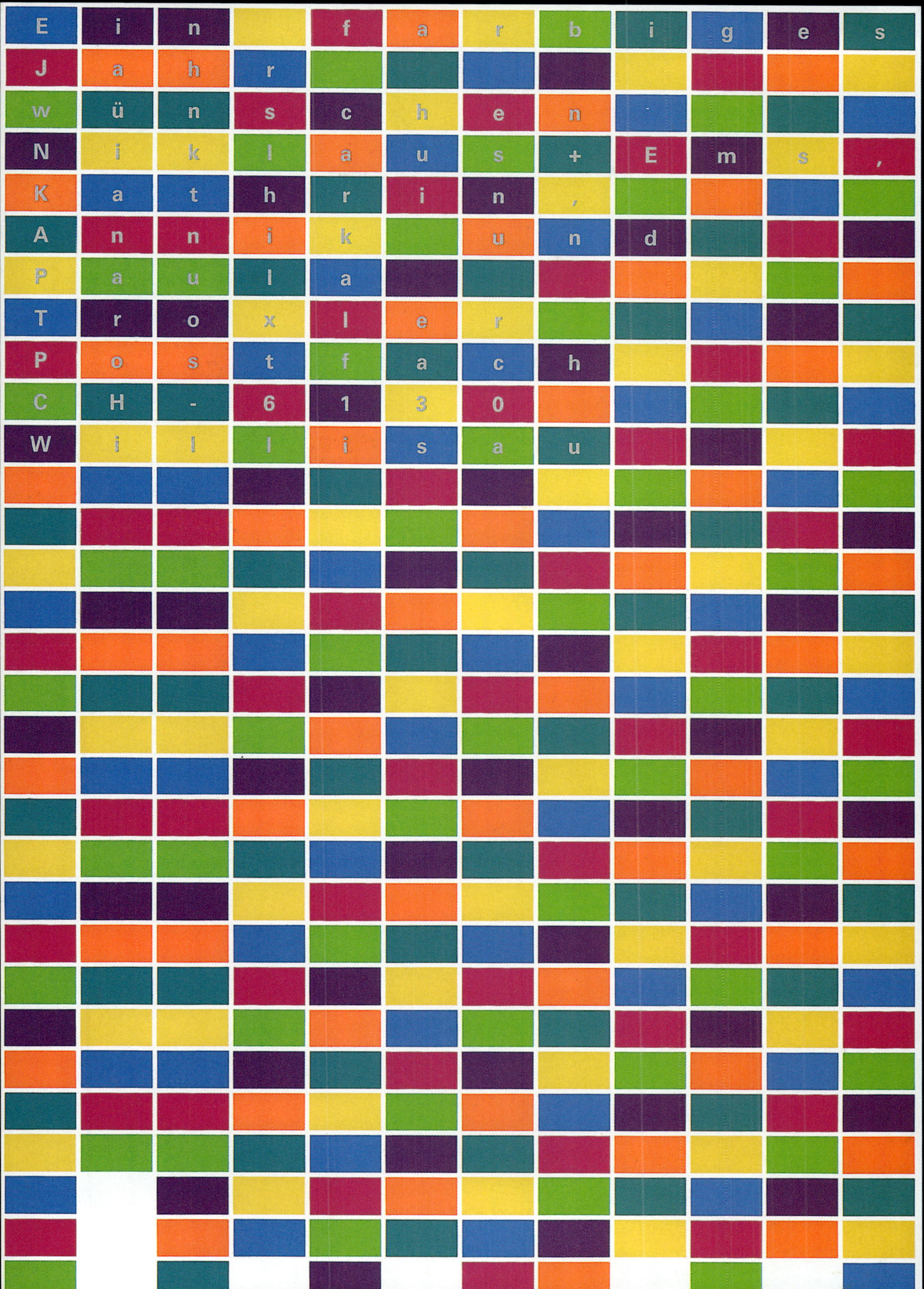

Ein farbiges
Jahr
wünschen
Niklaus + Ems,
Kathrin,
Annik und
Paul
Troxler
Postfach
CH-6130
Willisau

Designer **Niklaus Troxler** Client **Niklaus Troxler (New Year's card)**

Doug Carpenter
Brian Sullivan
are pleased to announce the formation of
CARPENTER/SULLIVAN
advertising, marketing, public relations

Design Firm **Elixir Design Inc.** Creative Director **Jennifer Jerde** Designers **Jennifer Jerde, Renee Toy, Nathan Durrant** and **Holly Holmquist** Photographer **Thomas Petillo** Copywriter **Stephanie Marlis** Client **Elixir Design**

(this spread) Design Firm **Corporate Edge** Creative Director **Matthew Renton** Designer **Aubrey Kurlansky** Photographer **Matthew Ward** Illustrators **Peter Horridge, David Lyttleton, Mike Hall, Anthony Williams** and **Stuart Simpson** Client **Corporate Edge**

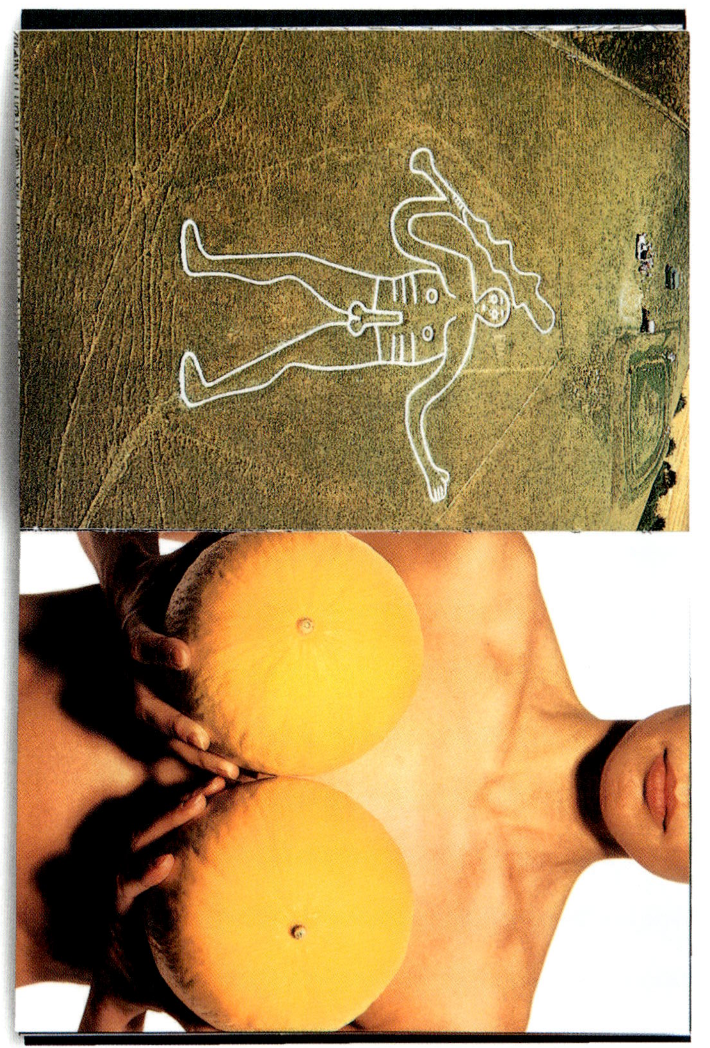

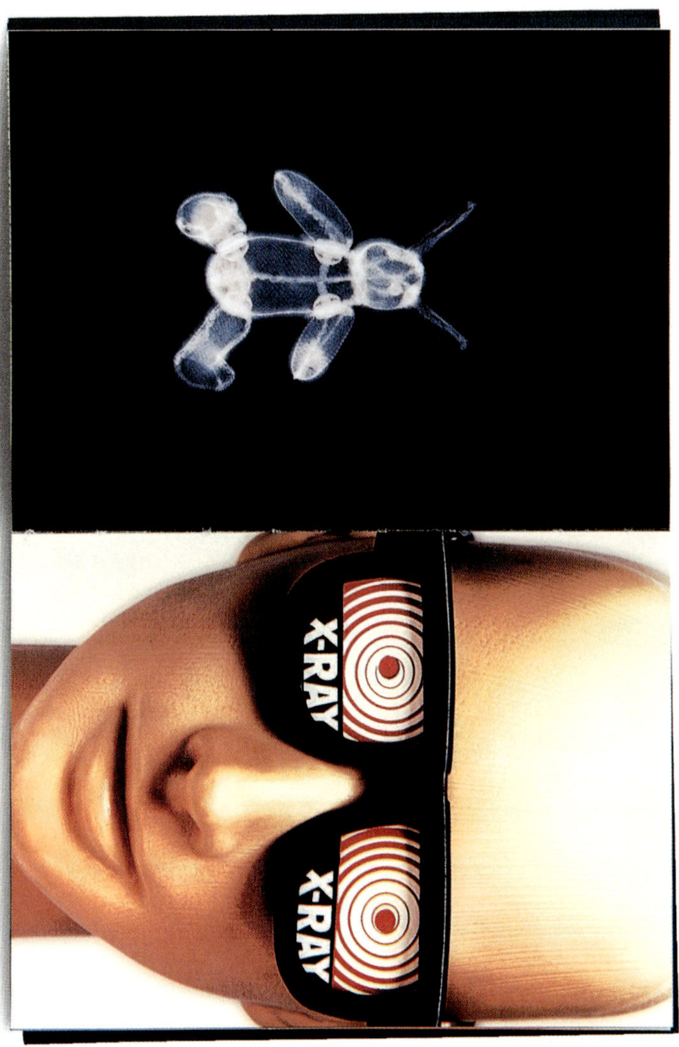

"HIS MASTER'S VOICE"
LONG PLAY
ALP.1186
The beautiful voice
Enrico Caruso
BEING20

MARCH
14
MARCH
15

INTIMIDATING
ACCUDART
Our new line of Hologram Flights
is sure to send a chill down
your opponent's spine!
You'll let out a cheer when
you see our complete line of
collegiate and NFL Team Flights!
Our new theme-oriented
Hologram Flights are sure to put
a charge in your game!
HAPPY FOURTH OF JULY
from your friends at Accudart
It's easy to fall in love with
our winter line of new Flights
and darting accessories.
HAPPY VALENTINE'S DAY

Client **Frost Design** (opposite) Design Firm **Sunspots Creative, Inc.** Art Director, Illustrator and Copywriter **Rick Bonelli** Designers **Rick Bonelli** and **Deena Hartle** Photographer **Manny Akis** Client **Accudart**

Design Firm **Frost Design** Creative, Art Director and Designer **Vince Frost**

SS Studio Art Director **Sayuri Shoji** Designers **Sayuri Shoji** and **Atsuko Suzuki** Photographer **Shu Akaski** Client **Issey Miyake, Inc.**

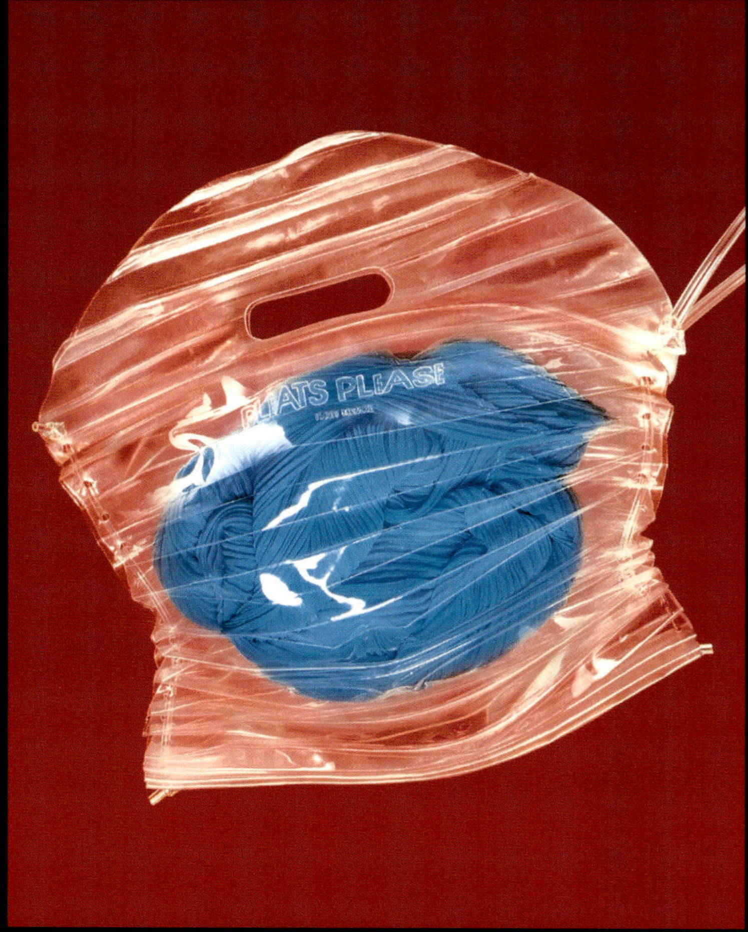

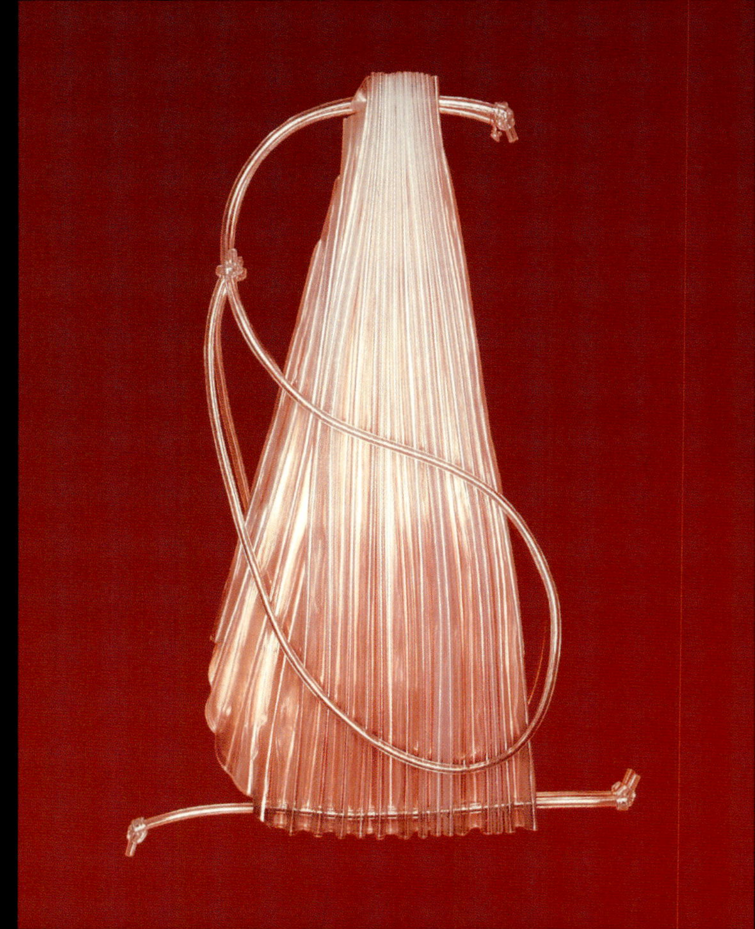

Design Firm **The Jupiter Drawing Room South Africa** Creative Director, Art Director and Designer **Joanne Thomas** Copywriter **Sanjai Mistry** Client **Young Designers Emporium (Y.D.E.)**

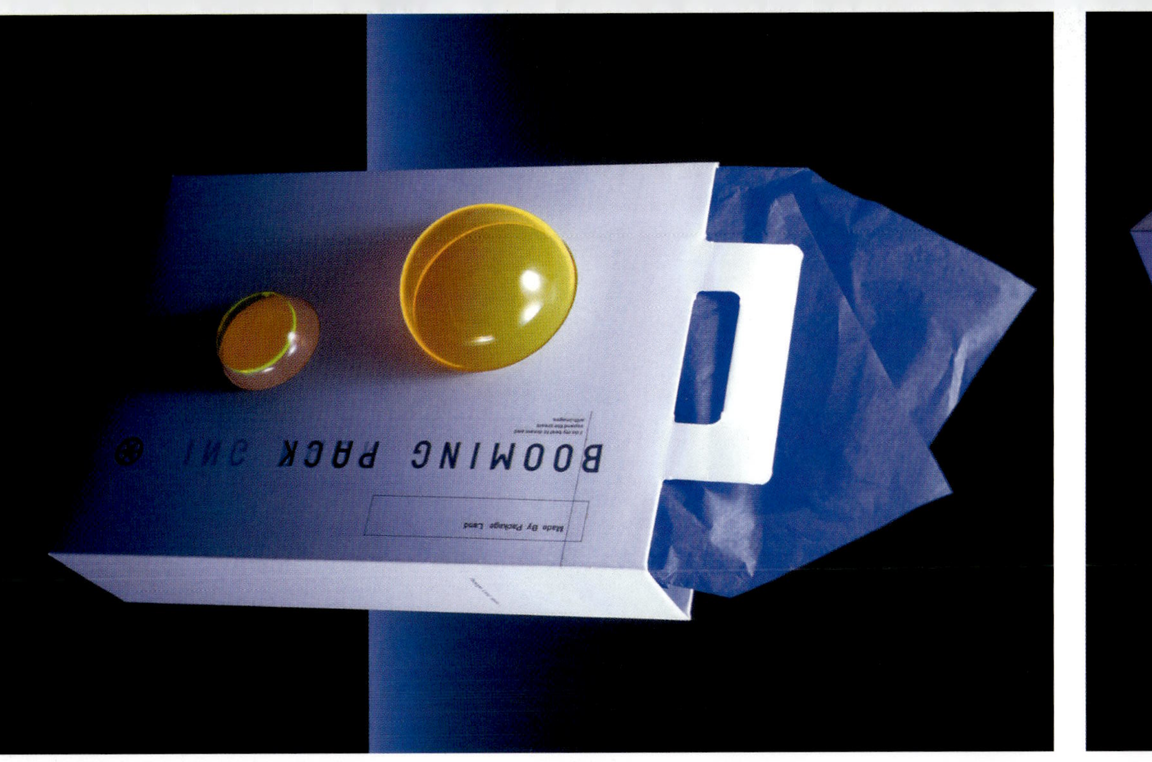

Design Firm **Package Land Co., Ltd.** Art Director, Designer and Photographer **Yasuo Tanaka** Client **Package Land Co., Ltd.**

FHA Image Design Creative Director, Art Director and Designer **FHA Image** Client **Australia Post** (middle) Design Firm **KROG** Art Director and Designer **Edi Berk** Client **Posta Slovenije, Maribor**

AMERICAN ILLUSTRATORS

rm **Fossil, Inc.** Creative Director **Tim Hale** Art Director **David Bates** Designers **John Vineyard** and **David Eden** Photographer **David McCormick** Client **Fossil, Inc.**

Design Firm **Frost Design** Creative Director, Art Director and Designer **Vince Frost** Client **Frost Design**

Design Firm **Art Force Studio** Art Director and Designer **Zoltan Halasi** Client **Nadai Studio**

Indices Verzeichnisse Index

Abare, Tim *Boulder, CO 303 444 4134* 217
Akay, Oguzhan *Istanbul, Turkey 90 21 22 619 518* 52
Akiyan, Kazuo *New York, NY 212 979 0300* 40
Allen, Kelly *Dallas, TX 214 922 9080* 171
Amano, Kazutoshi *Tokyo, Japan 81 33 538 2051* 173
Ambrosini, Ken *Portland, OR 503 223 9399* 156
Anderson, Gail *New York, NY 212 484 1665* 99, 101, 102
Anderson, Jack *Seattle, WA 206 467 5800* 163
Aparicio, Nicolas *San Francisco, CA 415 365 3723* 183
Apicella, Lorenzo *London, England 44 20 7 229 3477* 128, 129
Arebalo Jr., J. R. *Fort Worth, TX 817 967 2315* 106, 107
Arenas, Ivan *New York, NY 212 683 7000* 130, 131
Arnet, Craig *Irvine, CA 949 754 2073* 46, 47
Athorn, John *New York, NY 212 979 2661* 163

Barton, Mike *Irvine, CA 949 754 2073* 46, 47
Bates, David *Richardson, TX 972 699 2285* 240
Beatty, Chris *Boulder, CO 303 444 4134* 217
Beckerle, Matthew *Toronto, Canada 416 504 1367* 109
Bell, Ted *Horsham, PA 215 957 9871* 195
Bellamy, David *Boulder, CO 303 444 4134* 217
Berk, Edi *Ljubljana, Slovenia 38 61 426 5761* 238
Berresford, Lee *New York, NY 212 484 1665* 100
Biber, Jim *New York, NY 212 683 7000* 118, 130, 131
Birlew, Dan *Dallas, TX 214 987 6500* 160
Blankenship, Jeff *Memphis, TN 901 578 8055* 134, 135
Bone, Andy *London, England 44 20 7 837 8659* 164
Bonelli, Rick *Hoboken, NJ 201 459 9199* 232
Boswell, Joanne *London, England 44 20 7 855 5819* 42
Bottoni, Clint *New York, NY 212 473 2892* 48, 49
Boy Girl Boy *Wellington, New Zealand 64 04 499 0828* 140
Boynton, Richard *Minneapolis, MN 612 630 5138* 78
Braught, Mark *Decatur, GA 404 373 7430* 156
Brink, Gaby *San Francisco, CA 415 255 9295* 88, 89, 142, 152
Brinkman, Mark *Austin, TX 512 473 2333* 162
Britton, Patti *Sonoma CA 707 938 8378* 190
Brooks, Roy *New York, NY 212 683 7000* 130, 131
Budgen, Holly *London, England 44 20 7 837 8659* 164
Bunde, Nils *Chicago, IL 773 395 2500* 160
Butler, John *Sausalito, CA 415 331 6049* 176
Byrd, Rion *New York, NY 212 683 7000* 110, 111, 114, 115

Carnegie, Wendy *Austin, TX 512 476 3076* 212
Carpenter, Doug *Memphis, TN 901 725 9256* 228
Carr, Shelby *San Francisco, CA 415 896 0499* 30, 31
Carter, Brett *Austin, TX 512 476 3076* 201
Celic, Christine *Winston-Salem, NC 336 748 1364* 43
Cerveny, Lisa *Seattle, WA 206 467 5800* 163
Chan, Dominic *Causeway Bay, Hong Kong 85 228 609 688* 161
Chao, Alex *Santa Monica, CA 310 396 7724* 148
Chipchase, Jane *London, England 44 20 7 631 3370* 198
Chon, Dok *New York, NY 212 683 7000* 86, 87, 110, 111, 114, 115
Church, Stan *New York, NY 212 755 2903* 222
Church, Wendy *New York, NY 212 755 2903* 222
Cook, Deborah *Pasadena, CA 626 396 2200* 39
Cook, Susanna *London, England 44 20 7 611 5000* 77
Crawford, Emily *Boston, MA 617 624 9196* 109
Crisp, Denise Gonzales *Pasadena, CA 626 584 8417* 211
Crocker, Bruce *Brookline, MA 617 738 7884* 143
Curran, Fiona *London, England 44 20 7 255 3232* 175, 190
Cusson, Natalie *Toronto, Canada 416 979 4202* 76

De Mesties, Clementine *Paris, France 33 15 375 2644* 167
Decker, Lynda *New York, NY 212 633 8588* 226
Delago, Ken *New York, NY 212 484 1665* 98, 102, 103
Delana, Libby 158
Delaney, Kris *San Francisco, CA 415 255 9295* 88, 89
Demel, Rene *Eden Prarie, MN 952 942 6555* 68
Devendorf, Scott *New York, NY 212 683 7000* 130, 131
Donna, Tony *Culver City, CA 310 568 2450* 45
Dowling, John *London, England 44 20 7 229 3477* 80, 81
Duckworth, Bruce *San Francisco, CA 415 495 8691* 155
Durrant, Nathan *San Francisco, CA 415 834 0300* 82, 229

Eden, David *Richardson, TX 972 699 2285* 240
Edlefson, Brian *Zeeland, MI 616 654 8225* 70
Eisele, Yael *New York, NY 212 982 7621* 50, 72
Eko, Carrie *Austin, TX 512 473 2333* 19
Erb, Doug *Santa Monica, CA 310 449 2603* 168
Erhart, Marty *Austin, TX 512 242 5800* 163
Evans, Jon *Edinburgh, Scotland 44 131 553 5050* 192, 193
Evelock, James *Brookline, MA 617 738 7884* 143
Exquisite Corporation *San Francisco, CA 415 929 5100* 104, 105

Fadness, Matthew *San Francisco, CA 415 352 5848* 112, 113
Feigin, Piroyshkov *Moscow, Russia 70 95 961 8045* 156
Ferrero, Pablo *Buenos Aires, Argentina 54 114 783 7610* 132
FHA Image Design *Melbourne, Australia 613 9254 0254* 238
Flower, Brandy *Santa Monica, CA 310 449 2603* 168
Ford, Wayne *London, England 44 20 7 713 4212* 94, 95
Foster, Philip *San Francisco, CA 415 365 3723* 183
Fowler, Melanie *Fort Worth, TX 817 963 1903* 106
Fowler, Thomas G. *Norwalk, CT 203 845 0700* 225
Fox, Ken *Chicago, IL 312 895 5078* 63
Frankovic, Orsat *Dubrovnik, Croatia 38 59 112 35123* 60
Freach, Tanya *Dallas, TX 214 987 6500* 207
Frolick, Stuart I. *Pasadena, CA 626 584 8417* 211
Frost, Vince *London, England 44 20 7 490 7994* 90, 91, 199, 233, 241
Frykholm, Stephen *Zeeland, MI 616 654 8225* 70
Fujita, Makoto *Osaka, Japan 81 66 943 9077* 53
Fukui, Kenji *Osaka, Japan 81 66 943 9077* 53
Fukumoto, Yasuyo *Osaka, Japan 81 66 941 9618* 206

Ganton Jr., Brian *Cedar Grove, NJ 973 857 5099* 157
Ganton, Christopher *Cedar Grove, NJ 973 857 5099* 157
Garrigan, Laurie *San Francisco, CA 415 344 0990* 16
Georgiou, Soulla *London, England 44 20 7 611 5000* 77
Gerdes, Steve *Venice, CA 310 392 4849* 166
Gericke, Michael *New York, NY 212 683 7000* 12, 13
Gerritzen, Mieke *Amsterdam, The Netherlands 31 0 654711506* 23
Gibson, Dianne *Fort Worth, TX 817 967 2315* 106, 107
Gladstone, Ethan *Pasadena, CA 626 584 8417* 211
Glickfeld, Elizabeth *New York, NY 212 683 7000* 130, 131
Graziolo, Michael *New York, NY 212 989 5103* 38
Greenwood, Peter *Bath Avon, England 12 25 44 2634* 69
Grodal, Eia *Oslo, Norway 472 296 3900* 190
Groh, Nick *Santa Monica, CA 310 664 9100* 119
Grove, Jonathan *Boston, MA 617 542 2647* 20, 44
Gudbjartsdottir, Kristin Thora *Reykjavik, Iceland 562 1177* 160
Guillory, David *Austin, TX 512 473 2333* 159
Gumler, Rolando *Phoenix, AZ 602 495 1260* 160
Gunderson, Brian *San Francisco, CA 415 255 9295* 152
Guthrie, Michael *Memphis, TN 901 578 8055* 134, 135

Haase, Sibylle *Bremen, Germany 42 133 4980* 66
Hada, Motoko *New York, NY 212 647 1789* 169
Halasi, Zoltan *Budapest, Hungary 361 339 5348* 242
Hale, Tim *Richardson, TX 972 699 2285* 240
Hamlett, Phil *San Francisco, CA 415 344 0990* 21
Hamlin, Matt *New York, NY 212 633 8588* 226
Hamm, Garrick *London, England 44 20 7 255 3232* 174, 175, 190
Hardy, John *Omaha, NE 402 341 4807* 170
Hartle, Deena *Hoboken, NJ 201 459 9199* 232
Healey, Bill *Horsham, PA 215 957 9871* 195
Hebe, Reiner *Leonberg, Germany 71 523 0920* 74, 75, 202, 203
Heck, Matt *Austin, TX 512 473 2333* 159
Heil, Randy *Henderson, NV 702 564 4301* 159
Heller, Steven *New York, NY 212 481 9737* 136
Henderson, Hayes *Winston-Salem, NC 336 748 1364* 41, 43
Henneka, Dietmar *San Francisco, CA 415 677 0988* 25
Henson, Julie *Phoenix, AZ 602 495 1260* 160
Herrman, Carl 239
Hicks, James *New York, NY 212 683 7000* 130, 131
Hinrichs, Kit *San Francisco, CA 415 896 0499* 30, 31, 118, 125, 141, 184
Hirata, Suzuko *Fukuoka, Japan 92 622 5844* 178
Hirschfelder, Katja *Bremen, Germany 42 133 4980* 66, 186
Holdeman, Sherrie *Wichita, KS 316 262 0085* 189
Holdeman, Tracy *Wichita, KS 316 262 0085* 189
Holmquist, Holly *San Francisco, CA 415 834 0300* 82, 229
Holt, Suzanne *New York, NY 212 683 7000* 118, 130, 131
Honsell, Heiko *Radolfzell, Germany 49 77 329 70187* 61
Hope, Jane *Toronton, Canada 416 979 4202* 76
Howry, Jill *San Francisco, CA 415 433 2035* 51
Hurley, Foster *Albuquerque, NM 505 243 4000* 27
Hutchison, Mary Chin *Seattle, WA 206 467 5800* 163
Hynes, Bryan *Paramus, NJ 210 226 2960* 137

IBM Japan Design Center 204
Israel, Lonny *San Francisco, CA 415 352 5848* 112, 113

Jackson, Kelda *Baltimore, MD 410 563 2100* 56, 57
Jacobs, Brian *New York, NY 212 683 7000* 118, 141
Jerde, Jennifer *San Francisco, CA 415 834 0300* 82, 229
John-donnell, Riley *San Francisco, CA 415 929 5100* 104, 105

CreativeDirectorsArtDirectorsDesigners

Johnson, Amy *Portland, OR 503 241 9789* 149

Kato, Masaaki *Osaka, Japan 81 66 943 9077* 53
Kawamura, Tetsuji *Fukuoka, Japan 92 622 5844* 178
Kellerhouse, Neil *Venice, CA 310 392 4849* 166
Kellerman, Bob *Boston, MA 617 542 2647* 14
Kellum, Ron *New York, NY 212 979 2661* 163
Kilmer, Richard *Albuquerque, NM 505 260 1175* 189
King, Monica *St. Louis, MO 314 725 6616* 18
Klein, Richard *San Francisco, CA 415 929 5100* 104
Klim, Marcus *Avon, CT 860 678 1222* 190
Klim, Matt *Avon, CT 860 678 1222* 190
Knepfer, Rachel *New York, NY 212 484 1665* 98, 99, 100, 102, 103
Koppel, Terry *New York, NY 212 522 5152* 92, 93
Kudo, Aoshi *Tokyo, Japan 81 33 572 5111* 120, 121
Kuhlmann, Deanna *St. Louis, MO 314 725 6616* 18
Kurlansky, Aubrey *London, England 44 20 7 855 5819* 230, 231
Kuwano, Tetsuo *Osaka, Japan 81 66 943 9077* 53

LaCoste, Kerry *Boston, MA 617 542 2647* 14
Laidlaw, Tom *Boston, MA 617 542 2647* 20, 44
Laksmi, Anastasia *San Francisco, CA 415 365 3723* 183
Law, Vivian *Boston, MA 617 478 2470* 126, 127
Lenmann, Christopher *San Francisco, CA 415 365 3723* 183
Lerch, Liliane *San Francisco, CA 415 677 0988* 25
Levin, Lisa *San Francisco, CA 415 581 1529* 188
Lindner, John *Glen Allen, VA 804 968 7468* 224
Lippa, Domenic *London, England 44 20 87 442 100* 185
Louey, Robert *Santa Monica, CA 310 396 7724* 148
Lourme, Patrice *Paris, France 33 15 375 2644* 167

Machado, João *Porto Portugal 351 22 610 3772* 196, 197
Maier, Katja *Leonberg, Germany 71 523 0920* 74, 75
Marnich, Wladimir *Barcelona, Spain 34 93 208 1090* 84, 85
Marshall, Randall *Albuquerque, NM 505 260 1175* 189
Maruyama, Karl S. *Norwalk, CT 203 845 0700* 225
Matsumoto, Takaaki *New York, NY 212 807 0248* 64, 208
Matthews, Su *New York, NY 212 683 7000* 12, 13
Maurer, Mary *Santa Monica, CA 310 449 2603* 168
McAffrey, Terry 239
McClure, Tim *Austin, TX 512 242 5800* 83, 162
McDonald, Douglas *San Francisco, CA 415 896 0499* 141
McGinn, Michael *New York, NY 212 979 0300* 40
McMillan, Charlie *Westport, CT 203 227 8696* 116, 117
McMillan, Nancy *Westport, CT 203 227 8696* 116, 117
McMillen, Nancy *Austin, TX 512 476 3076* 35
Mejia, Gilberto *Fort Worth, TX 817 931 9984* 106, 107
Mergold, Alex *New York, NY 212 683 7000* 118
Merritt, Dennis *Irvine, CA 949 754 2073* 46, 47
Meyer, Anita *Boston, MA 617 478 2470* 126, 127
Meyer, Mirka *Frankfurt, Germany 1 739 301 091* 39, 54, 153
Michael, Anthony *London, England 44 20 7 631 3370* 198
Miki, Ken *Osaka, Japan 06 358 5270* 204, 205
Miller, J. Abbott *New York, NY 212 683 7000* 96, 97, 124, 130, 131
Milton, Laura *San Francisco, CA 415 344 0990* 21
Minkley, David *New York, NY 212 755 2903* 222
Minor, Dale *Austin, TX 512 242 5800* 83
Mir, Josep Maria *Barcelona, Spain 34 93 208 1090* 84, 85
Misawa, Shino *Tokyo, Japan 81 33 538 2051* 26, 172
Mitchell, Dick *Dallas, TX 214 987 6500* 156
Mitchell, Patrick *Boston, MA 617 624 9196* 109
Morton, Ann *Phoenix, AZ 602 495 1260* 160
Mues, Melanie *London, England 44 20 7 490 7994* 90, 91
Muller, Jennifer S. *New York, NY 212 522 5152* 92, 93
Munson, Milo *Henderson, NV 702 564 4301* 159
Murillo, Rolando *Dallas, TX 214 987 6500* 207
Muroga, Takayo *San Francisco, CA 415 896 0499* 30, 31
Murphy, Brandon *Dallas, TX 214 939 9194* 15
Murphy, Mark *Cleveland, OH 800 486 6275* 133
Mytton, Bob *Bath Avon, England 12 25 44 2634* 69

Nagai, Kazumasa *Tokyo, Japan 81 33 567 3232* 194
Nash, Stephanie *London, England 44 20 7 631 3370* 198
Nicolas, Gwenael *Tokyo, Japan 81 35 333 8525* 123
Niemann, Brian *Dallas, TX 214 265 0026* 144
Nolan, Patrick *Austin, TX 512 242 5800* 163
Nowicki, Larissa *New York, NY 212 807 0248* 64, 208
Nynas, Tom *Dallas, TX 214 987 6500* 154, 156, 160

O'Reilly, Brien *Norwalk, CT 203 845 0700* 225
O'Reilly, Erin *San Francisco, CA 415 352 5848* 112, 113
Oehler, Justus *London, England 44 20 7 229 3477* 34
Ohishi, Ichiji *Tokyo, Japan 81 33 538 2051* 26, 155
Okumura, Akio *Osaka, Japan 81 66 941 9618* 179, 206
Oldham, Emma *London, England 44 20 7 611 5000* 77
Olsen, Jon *Portland, OR 503 248 9466* 177, 180, 181
Olson, Tracy *Eden Prairie, MN 952 942 6555* 68
Omel, Andy *New York, NY 212 484 1665* 102
Onimaru, Toshihro *Tokyo, Japan 81 33 449 0651* 146, 147, 155, 159

Park, Min Hee *New York, NY 212 522 5152* 92
Peake, Kevin *Austin, TX 512 242 5800* 163
Pearce, Harry *London, England 44 20 87 442 100* 185
Pérez, Miguel *San Diego, CA 619 234 6631* 155, 159
Perkins, Robin *Santa Monica, CA 310 664 9100* 119, 191
Peteet, Rex *Austin, TX 512 473 2333* 19
Petersen, Mike *Chicago, IL 312 895 5078* 63
Pfeifer, Herbie *San Francisco CA 415 677 0988* 25
Polakov, Alexander *New York, NY 212 979 0300* 40
Pompard, Clare *London, England 44 20 7 255 3232* 174
Porter, John *New York, NY 212 683 7000* 130, 131
Primosch, Adrienne *Chicago, IL 312 895 5078* 63

Rage, Sean *Eden Prairie, MN 952 942 6555* 68
Ray, Scott *Dallas, TX 214 954 0522* 209
Regenbogen, Jeremy *San Francisco, CA 415 583 8447* 213
Reid, Judith *Edinburgh, Scotland 44 131 553 5050* 192, 193
Reiser, Jesse A. *Boston, MA 617 478 2470* 126, 127
Renton, Matthew *London, England 44 20 7 855 5819* 42, 230, 231
Reynolds, Terrance *Austin, TX 512 242 5800* 83
Ricardou, Antoine *Paris, France 33 15 375 2644* 167
Richards, Dan *Portland, OR 503 248 9466* 155
Richards, Todd *San Francisco, CA 415 433 2035* 51
Robrecht, Georgia *Santa Monica, CA 310 664 9100* 191
Roots, Jeremy *London, England 44 20 87 442 100* 185
Rushworth, John *London, England 44 20 7 229 3477* 80, 81
Rutka, Anthony *Baltimore, MD 410 563 2100* 56, 57
Ruyle, Wendy *Minneapolis, MN 888 590 4405* 62

Sagmeister, Stefan *New York, NY 212 647 1789* 169
Sahoh, Taku *Tokyo, Japan 81 33 538 2051* 172
Sakaida, Shigeyuki *Osaka, Japan 06 358 5270* 204, 205
Samuel, Derek *London, England 44 20 72 660 231* 32, 33
Sandstrom, Steve *Portland, OR 503 248 9466* 155, 177, 180, 181, 187
Sargent, Tricia *Eden Prarie, MN 952 942 6555* 68
Satoh, Taku *Tokyo, Japan 81 33 538 2051* 22, 26, 155, 172, 173, 200
Savasky, Julie *Austin, TX 512 476 3076* 55
Scheel, Alison *Atlanta, GA 404 347 9050* 159
Scher, Paula *New York, NY 212 683 7000* 86, 87, 110, 111, 114, 115, 118
Scheurer, Michelle *Eden Prairie, MN 952 942 6555* 68
Schmidt, Anders *Stockholm, Sweden 46 87 29 9600* 17, 165
Schmitt, Erik *San Francisco, CA 415 896 0499* 184
Schwartzott, Gretel *Brooklyn, NY 718 852 9711* 218, 219
Schweers, Harald *Bremen, Germany 42 133 4980* 186
Schwerzmann, Urs *San Francisco, CA 415 677 0988* 25
Sebastian, Jim *New York, NY 212 979 0300* 40
Serrano, José *San Diego, CA 619 234 6631* 155, 159
Shade, Suzanne *Sausalito, CA 415 331 6049* 176
Sharp, Amy *Memphis, TN 901 725 9256* 228
Shimamura, Takehiko *Tokyo, Japan 81 33 538 2051* 26
Shiokawa, Minoru *Tokyo, Japan 81 33 538 2051* 173
Shoji, Sayuri *Tokyo, Japan/New York, NY 212 765 0727* 214, 215, 223, 234, 235
Siu, Simon *Causeway Bay, Hong Kong 85 228 609 688* 161
Sodupe, Anna *Barcelona, Spain 34 93 208 1090* 84, 85
Spademan, Rob *Westport, CT 203 227 8696* 116, 117
Stayner, Don *Seattle, WA 206 467 5800* 163
Stone, Charles *Fort Worth, TX 817 967 3780* 107
Stout, D. J. *Austin, TX 512 476 3076* 35, 201
Strunk, Elliot *Winston-Salem, NC 336 748 1364* 43
Sugisaki, Shinnoske *Osaka, Japan 81 66 943 9077* 53
Suter, Fabienne *Zurich, Switzerland 41 14 87 4087* 58, 59
Suzuki, Atsuko *Tokyo, Japan/New York, NY 212 765 0727* 234, 235
Suzuki, Shinsuke *Osaka, Japan 81 66 943 9077* 53
Sweeney, James *Glen Allen, VA 804 968 7468* 224

Takada, Yukichi *Osaka, Japan 81 66 943 9077* 53
Tanaka, Yasuo *Osaka, Japan 60 6675 0138* 220, 221, 237
Templin, Joel *San Francisco, CA 415 255 9295* 88, 89, 142, 152
Terwilleger, Bret *Memphis, TN 901 578 8055* 134, 135
Thares, Scott *Minneapolis, MN 612 630 5138* 78
Thomas, Brad *San Francisco, CA 415 352 5848* 112, 113
Thomas, Joanne *Cape Town, South Africa 27 21 680 3200* 236
Throndsen, Morten *Oslo, Norway 472 296 3900* 190

CreativeDirectorsArtDirectorsDesigners

Tjaden, Uta *London, England 44 20 7 229 3477* ... 34
Tjia, Siung *New York, NY 212 484 1665* ... 99, 100
Tokuda, Yuji *Tokyo, Japan 81 35 551 4949* ... 24
Tony Chi & Associates *Santa Monica, CA 310 396 7724* ... 148
Toy, Renee *San Francisco, CA 415 834 0300* ... 229
Trantham, Andy *Winston-Salem, NC 336 748 1364* ... 41
Troen, Dardinelle *Portland, OR 503 223 9399* ... 156
Troxler, Niklaus *Willisau, Switzerland 041 970 2731* ... 227
Turner, David *San Francisco, CA 415 495 8691* ... 155
Turner, Steve *San Francisco, CA 415 344 0990* ... 16, 21

Uckusa, Rikiya *Tokyo, Japan 81 33 572 5111* ... 120, 121
Underwood, Rodney *Pittsburgh, PA 412 995 9500* ... 182

Valentine, Iain *Edinburgh, Scotland 44 131 553 5050* ... 192, 193
Vanderbyl, Michael *San Francisco, CA 415 583 8447* ... 71, 213
Vaughn, Rick *Albuquerque, NM 505 243 4000* ... 27
Vineyard, John *Richardson, TX 972 699 2285* ... 240
Vissat, David *Pittsburgh, PA 412 995 9500* ... 182
Volkmann, Jens *Radolfzell, Germany 49 77 329 70187* ... 61
Vucic, Ivana *Zagreb, Croatia 38 51 668 3881* ... 65

Walker, John *Philadelphia, PA 215 735 7380* ... 138
Wang, Andrea *New York, NY 212 683 7000* ... 118, 130, 131
Ward, Charlie *Wellington, New Zealand 64 04 499 0828* ... 37, 140
Warner, Jonathan *San Francisco, CA 415 495 8691* ... 155
Way, Danielle *Bath Avon, England 12 25 44 2634* ... 69
Weil, Daniel *London, England 44 20 7 229 3477* ... 80, 81
Whittlesey, Nancy *Minneapolis, MN 888 590 4405* ... 62
Wilcott, Erica *San Francisco, CA 415 583 8447* ... 71
Wilcox, Mark *Atlanta, GA 404 538 2343* ... 163
Williams, Allison *New York, NY 212 982 7621* ... 50, 72
Williams, J. P. *New York, NY 212 982 7621* ... 50, 72
Williams, Lowell *Austin, TX 512 476 3076* ... 55, 212
Wilson, Sharon *Eden Prairie, MN 952 942 6555* ... 68
Windelev, Morten *Copenhagen, Denmark 453 391 3327* ... 150, 151
Winzeuried, Stefan *Zurich, Switzerland 41 14 87 4087* ... 58, 59
Woesner, Clint *Santa Monica, CA 310 664 9100* ... 119
Wood, Tom *New York, NY 212 473 2892* ... 48, 49
Woodward, Fred *New York, NY 212 484 1665* ... 88, 29, 36, 98, 99, 100, 101, 102, 103, 139
Wou, Michael *Montreal, Canada 514 933 1222* ... 122
Wright, Simon *London, England 44 20 88 53 3028* ... 163
Wu, Six *London, England 44 20 7 229 3477* ... 80, 81

Yasin, Steve *McLean, VA 888 641 4949* ... 145
Yehia, Nona *Boston, MA 617 478 2470* ... 126, 127
Yerkes, Nancy *Grand Rapids, MI 616 942 2262* ... 2, 6
Yonemoto, Mayuko *Tokyo, Japan 81 35 333 8525* ... 123
Yonemura, Hiroshi *Tokyo, Japan 81 33 538 2051* ... 155
Yörük, Nejat Emrah *Istanbul, Turkey 90 21 22 619 518* ... 52
Yu, Garson *Hollwood, CA 323 860 3187* ... 210
Yukawa, Toru *Tokyo, Japan 81 33 449 0651* ... 4
Yurkew, Mark ... 158

Zweck-Bronner, Michael *New York, NY 212 683 7000* ... 118, 130, 131

PhotographersIllustrators

Akaski, Shu *Tokyo, Japan/New York, NY 212 765 0727* 234, 235
Akis, Manny *Hoboken, NJ 201 459 9199* 232
Allen, Kelly *Dallas, TX 214 922 9080* 171
Alston, Kwaku *New York, NY 212 522 5152* 92, 93
Anderson, Tim *Winston-Salem, NC 336 748 1364* 41

Ballard, Richard *New York, NY 212 522 5152* 93
Baptiste, Marc *New York, NY 212 522 5152* 92, 93
Barber, John *Minneapolis, MN 612 630 5138* 78
Barnes, Brian *Boston, MA 617 542 2647* 20
Bennet, Sue *Stockholm, Sweden 46 87 29 9600* 17
Bistrowitz, Leslie *Boston, MA 617 542 2647* 14
Bonelli, Rick *Hoboken, NJ 201 459 9199* 232
Borden, Harry *London, England 44 20 7 713 4212* 95
Borge, Richard *San Francisco, CA 415 255 9295* 88, 89
Bosshart, Ruedi *Zurich, Switzerland 41 14 87 4087* 58, 59
Braldts, Bradt *New York, NY 212 484 1665* 101
Brinkman, Mark *Austin, TX 512 473 2333* 162
Burke, Adrian *London, England 44 20 7 855 5819* 42

Carnegie, Wendy *Austin, TX 512 476 3076* 55, 212
Carter, Keith *Austin, TX 512 476 3076* 35
Chatterly, Jason *Pasadena, CA 626 396 2200* 39
Chirazi, Steffan *Santa Monica, CA 310 449 2603* 168
Clinch, Danny *New York, NY 212 647 1789* 169
Coley, Don *Paris, France 33 15 375 2644* 167
Cooke, Matt *London, England 44 20 7 855 5819* 42
Cosgrove, Dan *Memphis, TN 901 578 8055* 134, 135
Curran, Fiona *London, England 44 20 7 255 3232* 190
Cutler, Craig *New York, NY 212 473 2892* 48, 49

Davey, Andy *Santa Monica, CA 310 664 9100* 119
Davidson, Rob *Toronto, Canada 416 979 4202* 76
Davis, Doug *Dallas, TX 214 954 0522* 209
De Villiers, Patrice *London, England 44 20 7 713 4212* 95
Deblonde, Gaultier *London, England 44 20 7 713 4212* 94
Dobry, Scott *Omaha, NE 402 341 4807* 170
Dole, Jody *Horsham, PA 215 957 9871* 195
Douglas, Andrew *London, England 44 20 7 490 7994* 199

Ehrs, Bruno *Stockholm, Sweden 46 87 29 9600* 17
Evans, Livia *Pittsburgh, PA 412 995 9500* 182
Evelock, James *Brookline, MA 617 738 7884* 143

Fawsett, Katherine *London, England 44 20 7 837 8659* 164
Ferrero, Pablo *Buenos Aires, Argentina 54 114 783 7610* 132
Fletcher, Peter *Santa Monica, CA 310 449 2603* 168
Flower, Brandy *Santa Monica, CA 310 449 2603* 168
Foster, Jeff *Portland, OR 503 248 9466* 177
Foster, Paul *Portland, OR 503 241 9789* 149
Friel, Michael *San Francisco, CA 415 365 3723* 183

Gallery, Bill *Brookline, MA 617 738 7884* 143
Gentl & Hyers *New York, NY 212 982 7621* 50
Goldman, Gregg *St. Louis, MO 314 725 6616* 18
Graf, Michael *Toronto, Canada 416 504 1367* 109
Grassl, Anton *Santa Monica, CA 310 664 9100* 119
Griffith, Christopher *London, England 44 20 72 660 231* 32, 33
Gudnason, Torkil *San Francisco, CA 415 929 5100* 105
Guillory, David *Austin, TX 512 473 2333* 159

Hada, Motoko *New York, NY 212 647 1789* 169
Hall, Mike *London, England 44 20 7 855 5819* 230, 231
Hamilton, David *Wellington, New Zealand 64 499 0828* 37
Hansen, Hans *Bremen, Germany 42 133 4980* 66
Harley Davidson Archives *Chicago, IL 312 895 5078* 63
Hatt, Dominik *Leonberg, Germany 71 523 0920* 74, 75
Hebert, Bill *Zeeland, MI 616 654 8225* 70
Hedrich, Jim *San Francisco, CA 415 583 8447* 71
Heffernan, Terry *San Francisco, CA 415 896 0499* 30, 31
Heil, Randy *Henderson, NV 702 564 4301* 159
Hendler, Sandra *Philadelphia, PA 215 735 7380* 138
Hennessy, Thomas *San Francisco, CA 415 834 0300* 82
Herber, Karl *Minneapolis, MN 612 630 5138* 78
Hernandez, Paul *Santa Monica, CA 310 449 2603* 168
Herring, Liz *London, England 44 20 88 53 3028* 163
Hillier, Derek *London, England 44 20 7 631 3370* 198
Hirata, Suzuko *Fukuoka, Japan 92 622 5844* 178
Horridge, Peter *London, England 44 20 7 855 5819* 230, 231
Huber, Vic *Irvine, CA 949 754 2073* 46, 47
Hursley, Tim *San Francisco, CA 415 352 5848* 112, 113

Ilic, Mirko *New York, NY 212 481 9737* 136
Indresano, Michael *Boston, MA 617 542 2647* 44

Jones, Jeff *Venice, CA 310 392 4849* 166
Jordan, Josh *San Francisco, CA 415 929 5100* 104
Josepe, David M. *Tokyo, Japan 81 33 572 5111* 120, 121
Jost, Larry *Portland, OR 503 248 9466* 180, 181

Kacunic, Tomislav J. *Zagreb, Croatia 38 51 668 3881* 65
Keely, Dennis *Santa Monica, CA 310 449 2603* 168
Kellerhouse, Neil *Venice, CA 310 392 4849* 166
Kendall, Earl *Minneapolis, MN 612 630 5138* 78
Kessler, Grant *Fort Worth, TX 817 967 2315* 107
Klim, Greg *Avon, CT 860 678 1222* 190
Knight, Nick *London, England 44 20 7 713 4212* 94
Koenig, Franics *Leonberg, Germany 71 523 0920* 74, 75
Krämer, Peter *Austin, TX 512 473 2333* 19
Kuhnle & Knödler *Radolfzell, Germany 49 77 329 70187* 61
Kurigami, Kazumi *Tokyo, Japan 81 33 538 2051* 200

LaChapelle, David *New York, NY 212 484 1665* 99
Lamotte, Michael *San Francisco, CA 415 495 8691* 155
Lea, Tom *Dallas, TX 214 939 9194* 15
Lee, Juan *Cedar Grove, NJ 973 857 5099* 157
Levine, Ron *Montreal, Canada 514 933 1222* 122
Lim, Dan *Toronto, Canada 416 504 1367* 109
Lyons, David *New York, NY 212 755 2903* 222
Lyttleton, David *London, England 44 20 7 855 5819* 230, 231

Machado, João *Porto, Portugal 351 22 610 3772* 196, 197
Mahurin, Matt *New York, NY 212 484 1665* 139
Manson, Karen *Santa Monica, CA 310 449 2603* 168
Markus, Kurt *New York, NY 212 484 1665* 28, 29
Mateo-Cruz, Fermin *San Diego, CA 619 234 6631* 155
Mauss, Peter *New York, NY 212 683 7000* 86, 87, 110, 111, 114, 115
McCormick, David *Richardson, TX 972 699 2285* 240
McLeod, William Mercer *New York, NY 212 484 1665* 102
Miller, Diana *London, England 44 20 7 611 5000* 77
Minato, Seiji *Osaka, Japan 81 66 943 9077* 53
Mondino, Jean Baptiste *New York, NY 212 484 1665* 102
Motomatsu, Katsutoshi *Fukuoka, Japan 92 622 5844* 178
Murdich, Lon *Winston-Salem, NC 336 748 1364* 43
Mylius, Sebastian *Bath Avon, England 12 25 44 2634* 69

Nynas, Tom *Dallas, TX 214 987 6500* 154,156,160

Ockenfells III, Frank W. *New York, NY 212 522 5152* 92
Okawa, Shigeru *Osaka, Japan 06 358 5270* 204, 205
Onimaru, Tohsihro *Tokyo, Japan 81 33 449 0651* 147, 155
Ostroy, Alex *New York, NY 212 484 1665* 101

Padgett, Jamie *Westport, CT 203 227 8696* 116, 117
Peake, Kevin *Austin, TX 5122425800* 163
Persson, Roland *Stockholm, Sweden 468 729 9600* 165
Peteet, Rex *Austin, TX 512 473 2333* 162
Peterson, Bruce 158
Petillo, Thomas *San Francisco, CA 415 834 0300* 229
Phelps, Bill *Minneapolis, MN 888 590 4405* 62
Poynter, Phil *London, England 44 20 7 713 4212* 95
Purdum, Jim *Fort Worth, TX 817 967 2315* 106

Rascona, Rodney *Irvine, CA 949 754 2073* 46, 47
Rawles, Simon *London, England 44 20 7 713 4212* 95
Ray, Scott *Dallas, TX 214 954 0522* 209
Reich, Harald *Schwabisch, Germany 71 7192 7230* 216
Rohan *Venice, CA 310 392 4849* 166
Rubin, Ilan *New York, NY 212 982 7621* 72
Runion, Lee *Winston-Salem, NC 336 748 1364* 41

Sandstrom, Steve *Portland, OR 503 248 9466* 187
Scaraglino, Michael *New York, NY 212 755 2903* 222
Schaafsma, Phil *Grand Rapids, MI 616 942 2264* 2, 6
Scheel, Alison *Atlanta, GA 404 347 9050* 159
Schenk, Rocky *Santa Monica, CA 310 449 2603* 168
Scholler, Martin *San Francisco, CA 415 495 8691* 99, 155
Schubert, Niels *Leonberg, Germany 71 523 0920* 74, 75
Sebastian, Jim *New York, NY 212 979 0300* 40
Seliger, Mark *New York, NY 212 484 1665* 98, 99, 100, 102, 103
Seo, Takashi *Tokyo, Japan 81 35 551 4949* 24
Shoji, Sayuri *Tokyo, Japan/New York, NY 212 765 0727* 214, 215, 223, 224, 225

PhotographersIllustrators

Simpson, Stuart *London, England 44 20 7 855 5819* 230, 231
Sodupe, Anna *Barcelona, Spain 34 93 208 1090* 84, 85
Solin, Vanja *Zagreb, Croatia 38 51 668 3881* 65
Sorren, Joe *Cleveland, OH 800 486 6275* 133
Stevens, Bob *Irvine, CA 949 754 2073* 46, 47
Sugimoto, Hiroshi *New York, NY 212 807 0248* 208
Suzuki, Shinsuke *Osaka, Japan 81 66 943 9077* 53
Swimmer, Lara *San Francisco, CA 415 352 5848* 112, 113

Takada, Yukichi *Osaka, Japan 81 66 943 9077* 53
Tanaka, Yasuo *Osaka, Japan 66 675 0138* 220, 221, 237
Temme, Marty *Santa Monica, CA 310 449 2603* 168
Thymann, Klaus *Minneapolis, MN 612 630 5138* 78
Torres, Tony *London, England 44 20 7 611 5000* 77
Trebelcock, Bryan *Irvine, CA 949 754 2073* 46, 47

Vack, Tom *Frankfurt, Germany 69 242 4240* 67
Vamos, Harry *Culver City, CA 310 568 2450* 45

Ward, Matthew *London, England 44 20 7 855 5819* 230, 231
Warych, Jim *Zeeland, MI 616 654 8225* 70
Watson, Albert *New York, NY 212 484 1665* 100
Webber, Meggan *Austin, TX 512 476 3076* 55
Welch, Stephen Austin *San Francisco, CA 415 344 0990* 21
Wessel, Catherine *Santa Monica, CA 310 449 2603* 168
Weymouth, Michael *Boston, MA 617 542 2647* 14, 20, 44
White, Bruce M. *Boston, MA 617 478 2470* 126, 127
Wilcox, Mark *Atlanta, GA 404 538 2343* 163
Williams, Anthony *London, England 44 20 7 855 5819* 230, 231
Wou, Michael *Montreal, Canada 514 933 1222* 122

Yamamoto, Kazumasa *Osaka, Japan 06 358 5270* 204
Yarbrough, Carl *Fort Worth, TX 817 967 3780* 107
Yilmaz, Tamer *Istanbul, Turkey 90 21 22 619 518* 52

Zingarecci, Mark Dallas, TX 214 939 9194 15

Copywriters

Abare, Tim *Boulder, CO 303 444 4134* ... 217
Assenza, Tony *Culver City, CA 310 568 2450* ... 45

Baldwin, Bill *Dallas, TX 214 939 9194* ... 15
Bauleke, Ann *Minneapolis, MN 888 590 4405* ... 62
Beaman, Lindsay *San Francisco, CA 415 433 2035* ... 51
Benda, Penny *St. Louis, MO 314 725 6616* ... 18
Berry, Lessley *San Francisco, CA 415 255 9295* ... 88, 89
Bonelli, Rick *Hoboken, NJ 201 459 9199* ... 232
Bottoni, Clint *New York, NY 212 473 2892* ... 48, 49
Boyce, Rikki *Memphis, TN 901 578 8055* ... 134, 135
Bramson, Ian *McLean, VA 888 641 4949* ... 145
Byfield, Ted *Amsterdam, The Netherlands 31 0 654711506* ... 23

Carlin, Kim *Baltimore, MD 410 563 2100* ... 56, 57
Catlin, John *Grand Rapids, MI 616 942 2264* ... 2, 6
Cook, Deborah *Pasadena, CA 626 396 2200* ... 39
Courier & Weymouth Design *Boston, MA 617 542 2647* ... 14
Crellin, Martin *San Francisco, CA 415 677 0988* ... 25
Cressler, Rebecca *McLean, VA 888 641 4949* ... 145

Dillon, Leslee *Portland, OR 503 248 9466* ... 177, 180, 181

Emerson, Rick *Minneapolis, MN 888 590 4405* ... 62
Evans, Jon *Edinburgh, Scotland 44 131 553 5050* ... 192, 193
Evans, Max *Albuquerque, NM 505 243 4000* ... 27
Evans, P. *Edinburgh, Scotland 44 131 553 5050* ... 192, 193

Frasier, Margaret *Horsham, PA 215 957 9871* ... 195
Furr, John *Irvine, CA 949 754 2073* ... 46, 47

Gair, Andrew *Wellington, New Zealand 64 04 499 0828* ... 140
Gerberding, Liza *Venice, CA 310 392 4849* ... 166

Hebe, Reiner *Leonberg, Germany 71 523 0920* ... 74, 75, 202, 203
Henneka, Dietmar *San Francisco, CA 415 677 0988* ... 25
Hinrichs, Kit *San Francisco, CA 415 896 0499* ... 30, 31
Hirasuna, Delphine *San Francisco, CA 415 896 0499* ... 30, 31
Hofer, Doris *Zurich, Switzerland 41 14 87 4087* ... 58, 59
Holm, Dick *Zeeland, MI 616 654 8225* ... 70
Horvath, Rachel *Toronto, Canada 416 504 1367* ... 109
Hudson, Clay *Austin, TX 512 242 5800* ... 163
Hurley, Foster *Albuquerque, NM 505 243 4000* ... 27

Ignazi, Peter *Toronto, Canada 416 979 4202* ... 76
Irving, Doug *Austin, TX 512 473 2333* ... 19

Jorgensen, Scott *Minneapolis, MN 612 630 5138* ... 78

Kawamura, Tetsuji *Fukuoka, Japan 92 622 5844* ... 178
Kisman, Max *Amsterdam, The Netherlands 31 0 654711506* ... 23
Klein, Susan *Boston, MA 617 542 2647* ... 14
Köseoglu, Yigit *Istanbul, Turkey 90 21 22 619 518* ... 52

Langley, Michael *Dallas, TX 214 922 9080* ... 171
Lin, Jeremy *San Francisco, CA 415 929 5100* ... 105
Lipnowski, Gerry *Montreal, Canada 514 933 1222* ... 122

Malcolm, Clark *Zeeland, MI 616 654 8225* ... 70
Mariani, John *Fort Worth, TX 817 967 2315* ... 107
Marlis, Stephanie *San Francisco, CA 415 834 0300* ... 229
Meyer, Mirka *Frankfurt, Germany 1 739 301 091* ... 39, 54, 153
Michels, Nicole *Sausalito, CA 415 331 6049* ... 176
Minkley, David *New York, NY 212 755 2903* ... 222
Mistry, Sanjai *Cape Town, South Africa 27 21 680 3200* ... 236
Murray, Richard *London, England 44 20 7 255 3232* ... 175
Mylius, Hitch *Bath Avon, England 12 25 44 2634* ... 69

Perkins, Mark *Dallas, TX 214 922 9080* ... 171
Plazonja, Jonathan *Brookline, MA 617 738 7884* ... 143

Rant, Jon *San Francisco, CA 415 344 0990* ... 21

Sampson, Tim *Memphis, TN 901 725 9256* ... 228
Sandoz, Steve *Portland, OR 503 248 9466* ... 187
Schroeder, Patricia *Austin, TX 512 476 3076* ... 55
Sichterman, Jack *Chicago, IL 312 895 5078* ... 63
Silverman, Laura *New York, NY 212 982 7621* ... 50
Smith, Pat *London, England 44 20 7 855 5819* ... 42
Snyder, Linda *Glen Allen, VA 804 968 7468* ... 224
Suffnes, Dorit *Dallas, TX 214 954 0522* ... 209

Thompson, Chuck *Fort Worth, TX 817 967 2315* ... 106

Wasiliniuk, Tasha *Toronto, Canada 416 504 1367* ... 109
Weaver, Joan *Baltimore, MD 410 563 2100* ... 56, 57
Wertkin, Gerard C. *San Francisco, CA 415 896 0499* ... 30, 31
Wilkens, Dann *San Francisco, CA 415 255 9295* ... 142
Williford, Daniel *McLean, VA 888 641 4949* ... 145
Wilson, Connie *St. Louis, MO 314 725 6616* ... 18
Wood, John *Austin, TX 512 476 3076* ... 35
Wood, Tom *New York, NY 212 473 2892* ... 48, 49

Young, Steven *Winston-Salem, NC 336 748 1364* ... 43

Design Firms

Achtung! Achtung! *Zagreb, Croatia 38 51 668 3881* ... 65
Advertising, art & ideas ltd. *Zurich, Switzerland 41 14 87 4087* ... 58, 59
Ally *London, England 44 20 7 611 5000* ... 77
Ambrosini Design *Portland, OR 503 223 9399* ... 156
American Airlines Publishing *Fort Worth, TX 817 967 2315* ... 106, 107
American Way *Fort Worth, TX 817 931 9984* ... 106, 107
Anderson Partners *Omaha, NE 402 341 4807* ... 170
Archit-X *Brooklyn, NY 718 852 9711* ... 218, 219
Art Center College of Design *Pasadena, CA 626 396 2200* ... 39
Art Force Studio *Budapest, Hungary 361 339 5348* ... 242
Atelier Haase & Knels *Bremen, Germany 42 133 4980* ... 186

Be_poles *Paris, France 33 15 375 2644* ... 167
BGX Limited *Causeway Bay, Hong Kong 85 228 609 688* ... 161
Blattner Brunner *Pittsburgh, PA 412 995 9500* ... 182
Brainforest *Chicago, IL 773 395 2500* ... 160
Brann Richmond *Glen Allen, VA 804 968 7468* ... 224
Brian J. Ganton & Associates *Cedar Grove, NJ 973 857 5099* ... 157
Britton Design *Sonoma CA 707 938 8378* ... 190
Butler, Shine & Stern *Sausalito, CA 415 331 6049* ... 176

Catapult Strategic Design *Henderson, NV 702 564 4301* ... 159
Chaney, Nieman, Munson & Son *Henderson, NV 702 564 4301* ... 159
Corporate Edge *London, England 44 20 7 855 5819* ... 42, 230, 231
Creative activity design company *Toronto, Canada 416 504 1367* ... 109
Creative Soup, Inc. *Atlanta, GA 404 538 2343* ... 163
Crocker Inc. *Brookline, MA 617 738 7884* ... 143
Curisoity Inc. *Tokyo, Japan 81 35 333 8525* ... 123

D Design *London, England 44 20 72 660 231* ... 32, 33
Decker Design *New York, NY 212 633 8588* ... 226
Dentsu Inc. *Tokyo, Japan 81 35 551 4949* ... 24
Design Office *Pasadena, CA 626 584 8417* ... 211
Designframe *New York, NY 212 979 0300* ... 40
Direct Design Studio *Moscow, Russia 70 95 961 8045* ... 156
DNA Design Ltd. *Wellington, New Zealand 64 04 499 0828* ... 37, 140
Drive Communications *New York, NY 212 989 5103* ... 38

Einson Freeman Inc. *Paramus, NJ 210 226 2960* ... 137
Elixir Design Inc. *San Francisco, CA 415 834 0300* ... 82, 229
Estudio Ferrero *Buenos Aires, Argentina 54 114 783 7610* ... 132
Exquisite Corporation *San Francisco, CA 415 929 5100* ... 104, 105

Fast Company *Boston, MA 617 624 9196* ... 109
FHA Image Design *Victoria, Australia 613 9254 0254* ... 238
Finn Nygaard Design *Copenhagen, Denmark 45 70 260 809* ... 79
Fossil, Inc. *Richardson, TX 972 699 2285* ... 240
Four IV Design Consultants Ltd. *London, England 44 20 7 837 8659* ... 164
Frost Design *London, England 44 20 7 490 7994* ... 90, 91, 199, 233, 241
Full Service *Memphis, TN 901 725 9256* ... 228

Graphics and Designing Inc. *Tokyo, Japan 81 33 449 0651* ... 4, 146, 147, 155, 159
Greenwich Design Associates *London, England 44 20 88 53 3028* ... 163
Griffith Phillips Creative *Dallas, TX 214 265 0026* ... 144
GSD&M *Austin, TX 512 242 5800* ... 83, 163

Haase & Knels *Bremen, Germany 42 133 4980* ... 66
HEBE Werbung & Design *Leonberg, Germany 71 523 0920* ... 74, 75, 202, 203
Heine/Lenz/Zizka *Frankfurt, Germany 69 242 4240* ... 67, 73
Henderson Tyner Art Co. *Winston-Salem, NC 336 748 1364* ... 41, 43
Hendler Inc. *Philadelphia, PA 215 735 7380* ... 138
Herman Miller Inc. *Zeeland, MI 616 654 8225* ... 70
Hornall Anderson Design Works, Inc. *Seattle, WA 206 467 5800* ... 163
Howry Design Associates *San Francisco, CA 415 433 2035* ... 51
Hvita Husid *Reykjavik, Iceland 562 1177* ... 160

Insight Design Communications *Wichita, KS 316 262 0085* ... 189
Intellecta Corporate *Stockholm, Sweden 46 87 29 9600* ... 17, 165

João Machado Design, Lda. *Porto, Portugal 351 22 610 3772* ... 196, 197
Jupiter Drawing Room *Cape Town, South Africa 27 21 680 3200* ... 236

Kellerhouse, Inc. *Venice, CA 310 392 4849* ... 166
Kellum McClain, Inc. *New York, NY 212 979 2661* ... 163
Ken Miki & Associates *Osaka, Japan 06 358 5270* ... 204, 205
Kilmer & Kilmer *Albuquerque, NM 505 260 1175* ... 189
Klim Design, Inc. *Avon, CT 860 678 1222* ... 190
KROG *Ljubljana, Slovenia 38 61 426 5761* ... 238

Landor Associates *Irvine, CA 949 754 2073* ... 46, 47
Landor Associates *San Francisco, CA 415 365 3723* ... 183
Larsen Design & Interactive *Minneapolis, MN 888 590 4405* ... 62
Levin Breidenbach Wade *San Francisco, CA 415 581 1529* ... 188
Lift Communications, Inc. *Portland, OR 503 241 9789* ... 149
Lippa Pearce Design Ltd. *London, England 44 20 87 442 100* ... 185
Louey/Rubino Design Group Inc. *Santa Monica, CA 310 396 7724* ... 148

M/W *New York, NY 212 982 7621* ... 50, 72
M:C Design Phx:Ffm *Frankfurt, Germany 1 739 301 091* ... 54, 153
Matsumoto Inc. *New York, NY 212 807 0248* ... 64, 208
McMillan Group Inc. *Westport, CT 203 227 8696* ... 116, 117
Michael Nash Associates *London, England 44 20 7 631 3370* ... 198
Mieke Gerritzen *Amsterdam, The Netherlands 31 0 654711506* ... 23
Miravo Communications *McLean, VA 888 641 4949* ... 145
Mires Design, Inc. *San Diego, CA 619 234 6631* ... 155, 159
Mirko Ilic Corp. *New York, NY 212 481 9737* ... 136
Montgomery & Pfeifer *San Francisco, CA 415 677 0988* ... 25
Movida Plus Map *Istanbul, Turkey 90 21 22 619 518* ... 52
Murphy Design Inc. *Cleveland, OH 800 486 6275* ... 133
Mytton Williams *Bath Avon, England 12 25 44 2634* ... 69

Navy Blue Design *Edinburgh, Scotland 44 131 553 5050* ... 192, 193
NDW Communications *Horsham, PA 215 957 9871* ... 195
Nippon Design Center, Inc. *Tokyo, Japan 81 33 567 3232* ... 194

Observer London, England *44 20 7 713 4212* ... 94, 95
Oden Marketing and Design *Memphis, TN 901 578 8055* ... 134, 135
Oliver Kuhlmann *St. Louis, MO 314 725 6616* ... 18
Origami Communication Design *Montreal, Canada 514 933 1222* ... 122
Orsat *Dubrovnik, Croatia 38 59 112 35123* ... 60
Ottenwälder und Ottenwälder *Schwabisch, Germany 71 7192 7230* ... 216

P.P.I.C. *Fukuoka, Japan 92 622 5844* ... 178
Package Land Co., Ltd. *Osaka, Japan 06 6675 0138* ... 220, 221, 237
Packaging Create Inc. *Osaka, Japan 81 66 941 9618* ... 179, 206
Pentagram Design *New York, NY 212 683 7000* ... 12, 13, 86, 87, 96, 97, 110, 111, 114, 115, 118, 124, 130, 131
Pentagram Design *San Francisco, CA 415 896 0499* ... 30, 31, 125, 141, 184
Pentagram Design Ltd. *London, England 44 20 7 229 3477* ... 34, 80,81,128,129
Pentagram Design, Inc. *Austin, TX 512 476 3076* ... 35, 55,201,212
Peterson & Company *Dallas, TX 214 954 0522* ... 209
Plus Design Inc. *Boston, MA 617 478 2470* ... 126, 127

RBMM *Dallas, TX 214 987 6500* ... 154, 156, 160, 207
re:public *Copenhagen, Denmark 453 391 3327* ... 150, 151
Rolling Stone Magazine *New York, NY 212 484 1665* ... 28, 29, 36, 98, 99, 100, 101, 102, 103, 139
Rutka Weadock Design *Baltimore, MD 410 563 2100* ... 56, 57

Sagmeister Inc., *New York, NY 212 647 1789* ... 169
Sandstrom Design *Portland, OR 503 248 9466* ... 155, 177, 180, 181,187
Seasonal Specialties In-House Design *Eden Prairie, MN 952 942 6555* ... 68
Selbert Perkins Design *Santa Monica, CA 310 664 9100* ... 119, 191
Shinnoske Inc. *Osaka, Japan 81 66 943 9077* ... 53
Shiseido Co. Ltd. *Tokyo, Japan 81 33 572 5111* ... 120, 121
Sibley Peteet Design *Austin, TX 512 473 2333* ... 19, 159, 162
Skidmore Owings & Merrill LLP *San Francisco, CA 415 352 5848* 112, 113
Sony Music *Santa Monica, CA 310 449 2603* ... 168
Squires & Company *Dallas, TX 214 939 9194* ... 15
SS Studio *Tokyo, Japan/New York, NY 212 765 0727* .. 214, 215, 223, 234, 235
Stamp Development Office ... 239
Stromme Throndsen Design *Oslo, Norway 472 296 3900* ... 190
Sullivan Perkins *Dallas, TX 214 922 9080* ... 171
Summa *Barcelona, Spain 34 93 208 1090* ... 84, 85
Sunspots Creative, Inc. *Hoboken, NJ 201 459 9199* ... 232

Taku Satoh Design Office Inc. *Tokyo, Japan 81 33 538 2051* ... 22, 26, 155, 172, 173, 200
TAXI *Toronto, Canada 416 979 4202* ... 76
Templin Brink Design *San Francisco, CA 415 255 9295* ... 88, 89, 142,152
Thinking Caps *Phoenix, AZ 602 495 1260* ... 160
Time Inc. Custom Publishing *New York, NY 212 522 5152* ... 92, 93
Tom Fowler, Inc. *Norwalk, CT 203 845 0700* ... 225
Turner & Associates *San Francisco, CA 415 344 0990* ... 16, 21
Turner Duckworth *San Francisco, CA 415 495 8691* ... 155

Vanderbyl Design *San Francisco, CA 415 583 8447* ... 71, 213
Vaugh Wedeen Creative *Albuquerque, NM 505 243 4000* ... 27
Volcano Design *Culver City, CA 310 568 2450* ... 45
VSA Partners, Inc *Chicago, IL 312 895 5078* ... 63

Wallace Church, Inc. *New York, NY 212 755 2903* ... 222

Design Firms

Weymouth Design *Boston, MA 617 542 2647* 14, 20, 44
Williams Murray Hamm *London, England 44 20 7 255 3232* ..174, 175, 190
Wink *Minneapolis, MN 612 630 5138* 78
Wood Design *New York, NY 212 473 2892* 48, 49
Workhorse Advertising *Boulder, CO 303 444 4134* 217
Yellobee Studio *Atlanta, GA 404 347 9050* 159
Yerkes Design *Grand Rapids, MI 616 942 2264* 2,6
yU+co *Hollwood, CA 323 860 3187* 210

Clients

2wice Arts Foundation 96, 97
770 Broadway/Wanamaker Building 86, 87
800.com 155

Accudart 232
Advertising, art & ideas ltd. 58, 59
Alexandra Von Der Beeck 37
American Institute of Graphic Arts (AIGA) 125
American Museum of Natural History 118
Ameristar Casinos 18
Amoco 137
Andante 167
Andrew Douglas 199
Art Center College of Design 211
Art Museum, Princeton University 126, 127
Asahi Satellite Broadcasting Limited 155
Association of Icelandic Insurance Companies 160
Athorn Clark & Partners 163
Austin Museum of Art 212
Australia Post 238

B.T. Dibbern GmbH & Co. KG 66
Barton Creek Country Club 162
Bellwether Exploration Company 15
Best Feeds 182
Blonde Magazine 109
Bols Royal Distilleries 190
Borrelli 155
Brann Richmond 224
Buchanan Visual Communications 144

Cambridge Carpet 163
Castor & Pollux Pet Products 180, 181
Catapult 159
Chase Food Company 159
Coleman Company 183
Corporate Edge 230, 231
Courier Corporation 14
Craig Cutler 48, 49
Crocker Inc. 143
CTD Capita 42

D&AD 90, 91
D. J. Stout 201
DACG 55
DaimlerChrysler AG 25
Dallas Public Library 171
Dallas Society of Visual Communications 209
Dentsu Inc. 24
Designtex 40
Domaine Haleaux 156
DWL 160

Elixir Design 229
Emperor Multimedia Limited 210
Entertainment Weekly Magazine 138
Epix Medical 20
Eurobubblies 191
Eventra 225
Exhibitor Magazine 213
Experience Music Project 112, 113

Farmhouse Web Company 152
Fossil, Inc. 240
Frost Design 233, 241
Full Service 228

Gabinete Deapoio Empressarial Do Vale Do 196, 197
Gap 39
George's Furniture Co., Ltd. 159
Gold Circle Entertainment 170
GSL Properties 156
Guggenheim Museum 64, 208
Gus Berthold Electric Company 160

Half Moon Catering 149
Halfords Limited 185
Hanes Printables 41, 43
Harley-Davidson 63
HBF 71
Heals Department Store 190
Heiwa Paper Co., Ltd. 205
Hennegan 48, 49
Herman Miller Inc. 2, 6, 70
Hermitage Road 190
Hitachi Maxell, Ltd. 4
Hitch Mylius 69
Hollywood Entertainment 177
Howry Design Associates 51
Hubbard Publicity 156

IBM Japan, Ltd. 204
Indian Motorcycle 142
Intellecta AB 17
Inter Medium Institute Graduate School 179
International Paper 134, 135
Issey Miyake, Inc. 123, 223, 234, 235

Japan Graphic Designers Association Inc. 22
Joe Sorren 133

Keith Carter 35
Kilmer & Kilmer 189
Knoll 226
Kosma Heinrich Kossman AG/Germany 216

Larsen Design & Interactive 62
Leica Camera AG 67
Lincoln Mercury 46, 47
Lionsgate Communications 160
Loews Cineplex 12, 13
Los Angeles World Airport 119

Maas Goldsmith 74, 75
Macromedia, Inc. 21
Marconi Medical Systems 116, 117
Mariela Goldin-La Caja ART SA 132
Maryland Institute, College of Art 56, 57
Mead Corporation 44
Messe Frankfurt 73
Miquel Alimentacio 84, 85
Miravo Communications 145
Mirka Meyer 153
Mother Hen Software 159
Movida Plus Map 52
Muzack 118

Nadai Studio 242
Nakashima Chochin Co. Ltd. 178
NapaStyle 184
National Portrait Gallery, London 164
Natural History Museum 128, 129
New 42nd Street Development 114, 115
New Art Gallery 198
New Jersey Performing Arts Center 110, 111
New York Times Book Review 136
Niklaus Troxler 227
Nokia (Hong Kong) 161
Nomi Restaurant 148
Nuance 176

Observer 94, 95
ODS 147, 155
Oriental Land Co., Ltd. 146
Orsat Frankovic 60
Osaka 2008 Olympic Bid Committee 53

P.G.C.D. Japan Inc. 172
Package Land Co., Ltd. 220, 221, 237

Clients

Palm Inc. 155
Pangea 54
Pantone 80, 81
Pharmacopia 188
Posta Slovenije, Maribor 238
Powerhouse Books Ltd. 34
Public Executions 154

Quiver Inc. 88, 89

Radioactive Records 169
Rams (High School Basketball Team) 156
Reprise Records. A Time Warner Company 166
Ringnes 190
Rock & Roll Hall of Fame & Museum 124
Rolling Stone Magazine 139
Ron Levine, Michael Wou 122

Saga Furs 150, 151
SAS (Scandinavian Airlines) 165
Schuhhaus Werdich GmbH & Co. 202, 203
Seasonal Specialties 68
Shell Aviation 163
Shiseido Co. Ltd. 120, 121, 173
Sony Electronics 92, 93
Sony Style 72
Southwest Airlines 83, 107
Space 77
Stanwell Vertriebs GmbH 186
Starlight Publishing 27
Stelton 79
Sterling Group/Sephora 214, 215
Stova/Enzo 45
Strathmore Papers and GF Smith 192, 193
Superdrug 174, 175
Surface Magazine 104, 105
Suzanne George 82

Takashimaya New York 50
Takeo Co., Ltd. 194
Target 78
Tazo 187
Telecom New Zealand 140
Textile-Technology Faculty, Zagreb 65
Theme Park 163
Tokyo Art Directors Club 26, 200
Tor Books 38
Triclops 160
Tropical Sportswear International 19
Twelve Horses 163

United States Postal Service 239
United States Tobacco International 157
University of Southern California 141
USA Film Festival 207

Virtu 76

Wallace Church Inc. 222
With A Twist 189
Workhorse Advertising 217

X'i an Image Playbill exhibition organization commitee 206

Yahoo! 16
Yellow Pages 159
Young Designers Emporium (Y.D.E.) 236
Yucos 156

Zanders USA 195

Graphis Publications

Advertising Annual 2001
Annual Reports 7
Poster Annual 2000
Book Design 2
Design Annual 2001
New Talent Design Annual 2000
"Caution: don't read this book unless you want to change your life. On the other hand, if you have work published here... pack your bags; you're already on your way."
Interactive Design 1
Corporate Identity 3
Packaging Design 8

Graphis Titles Available

Advertising Annual 2000
Advertising Annual 2001
Animal by James Balog
Annual Reports 7
Berko: Photographs 1935-1951
Black & White Blues
Book Design 2
Brochures 4
Corporate Identity 3
Design Annual 2001
Digital Photo 1
Interactive Design 2
Letterhead 5
Logo 5
Icograda: Masters of the 20th Century
New Talent Design 1999
New Talent Design 2000
New Talent Design 2001
Nudes 1 (Cloth)
Nudes 1 (Paper)
Nudes 3
Packaging 8
Pete Turner: African Journey
Photo Annual 2000
Photo Annual 2001
Poster Annual 1998
Poster 2000
Poster 2001
Product Design 2
Something to be Desired: Essays
on Design by Veronique Vienne
T-Shirt Design 2
The Graphic Art of Michael Schwab
Tintypes by Jane Hinds Bidaut
Top Ten in Advertising
Unspecial Effects for Graphic
Designers by Bob Gill
Walter Iooss: A Lifetime of
Shooting Sports & Beauty

At fine booksellers everywhere
or order at www.graphis.com

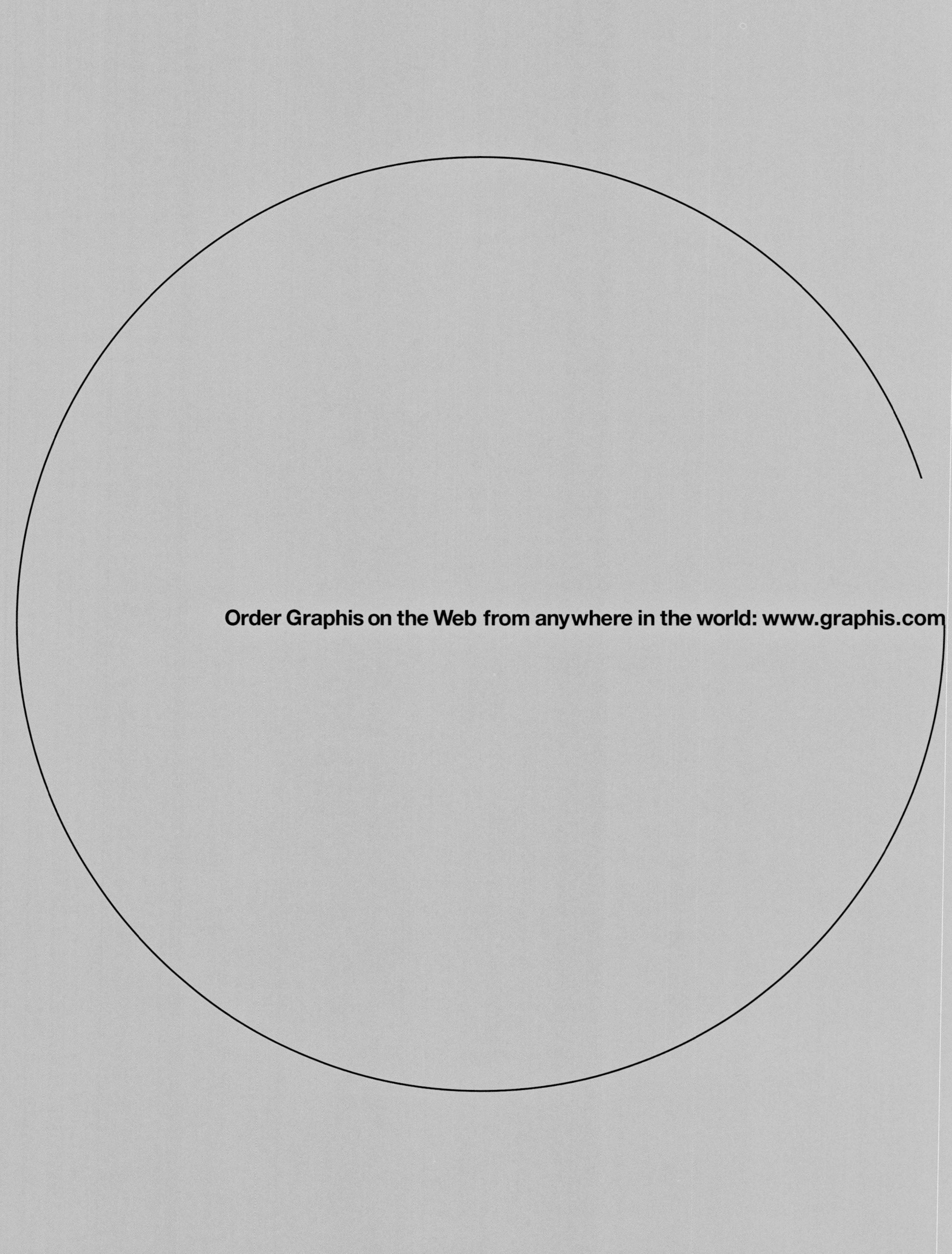